W9-BKI-650

CONSULTING ENGINEERING PRACTICE MANUAL

Edited by
Stanley Cohen

Editor of *Consulting Engineer* Magazine

Sponsored by
AMERICAN CONSULTING ENGINEERS COUNCIL

McGraw-Hill Book Company
New York • St. Louis • San Francisco • Auckland • Bogotá
Hamburg • Johannesburg • London • Madrid • Mexico
Montreal • New Delhi • Panama • Paris • São Paulo
Singapore • Sydney • Tokyo • Toronto

Library of Congress Cataloging in Publication Data
Main entry under title:

Consulting engineering practice manual.

  Includes index.
  1. Engineering—Handbooks, manuals, etc.
2. Consulting engineers—Handbooks, manuals, etc.
I. Cohen, Stanley, date.   II. American
Consulting Engineers Council.
TA157.0618   620'.0068   81-7282
                                                              AACR2
ISBN 0-07-001352-7

  34567890   DODO   898765432

The editors for this book were Joan Zseleczky and Diane Krumrey,
the designer was Jules Perlmutter (Off-Broadway Graphics),
and the production supervisor was Sally Fliess.
It was set in Century Schoolbook by Datapage.

Printed and bound by R.R. Donnelley.

*The pronouns "he" and "his" have sometimes been used in a purely generic sense
in this book to accommodate the text to the limitations of the English language
and avoid awkward grammatical constructions.*

TABLE OF CONTENTS

PREFACE

William R. Ratliff
President, American Consulting Engineers Council

Engineering students often spend years determining which disciplinary branch of engineering to pursue in their careers: aeronautical, chemical, civil, electrical, mechanical, mining, structural, environmental—and the list keeps growing. However, few students take the time to consider how they will apply these technical skills.

Generally, members of the learned professions are engaged in private practice, offering their services directly to clients or patients. As a result, most people are acquainted with the professions of law, medicine, and even architecture. Most engineers, on the other hand, furnish their services to an employer, such as a governmental agency, an industrial concern, or a construction company. Consequently, few people have a real understanding of the learned profession of consulting engineering.

The intent of this book is to acquaint the reader with consulting engineering as a career. It will endeavor to impart a sense of the challenges to be met in this field, as well as some of the opportunities and rewards that await engineers who might choose this avenue of applying their technical training.

Consulting engineers are unique to their profession in that they are required to be, in the jargon of the sports world, triple threats. They must be technically qualified in their disciplinary branch of engineering, they must maintain the high standards of conduct that are expected of professionals, and they must be capable of managing a business enterprise so that it returns a profit.

Technical competence is critical to consulting engineers, since that is the product they are selling. A sound reputation for quality design expertise is, of course, the first essential. It enables a firm to keep the clients it has and to obtain new ones, thus assuring a reasonably steady backlog of work. Without a flow of new projects, there will be no business to run, and even professionalism will be a commodity without a market value.

Still, technical competence, though necessary, is not of itself sufficient. Professionalism is of extreme importance to consulting engineers because of their relationship with their clients and with the public at large. Consulting engineers owe a fiduciary duty to their clients to fill their needs and represent them without conflict of interest. As professionals serving the public, they must be registered by the states in which they practice and bear a responsibility to protect the health, safety, and welfare of the general public.

Not least, consulting engineers must be effective business managers. Since their services are furnished to clients for a fee, they need to be able to manage money and run their firms on a sound economic basis. Neither extraordinary technical prowess nor lofty professional ideals will keep engineers in private practice very long if they are unable to market their services, to contract for those services in prudent terms, to manage the production of the work product contracted for, to charge and collect adequate fees, and to manage the assets that accrue from the business.

The nine chapters that follow were written by some of the leading consulting engineers in the United States. Together, they comprise a manual of practice with the aim of acquainting engineering students with virtually every aspect of the profession.

Included in the text is a description of some of the many and varied types of projects on which consulting engineers may work, along with a discussion of the technical disciplines that must all come together in any complex project. There is a chapter on the various types of clients that a consulting engineer might serve and an analysis of the client-engineer relationship. Professional liability, which is a concomitant of this business, is explained, as are the many aspects of operating an engineering office, including staffing, organization, personnel policies, computerization, fees, accounting, and cash flow.

How do consulting engineers obtain clients? The chapter devoted to that subject covers marketing, proposals, and the role of public relations. International practice—performing projects in foreign countries—is a vast and challenging field that is given a chapter's discussion. Professionalism, and the responsibilities it entails, is considered, along with an engineer's relationship with other professionals.

The last chapter is an introduction to American Consulting Engineers Council, a national organization consisting of about 10,000 owners and operators of engineering firms who have chosen to make their careers in consulting practice. ACEC, which is twenty-five years old this year, sponsored the production of this book to commemorate its Silver Anniversary and to educate the reader and student about the learned profession of consulting engineering.

Chapter

THE WORK OF THE CONSULTING ENGINEER

Leonard K. Crawford
Chairman of the Board, Crawford, Murphy & Tilly, Inc.

His location may be near the ocean, mountains, farmland, or megalopolis. His interest may lie in working with a billion-dollar industry, designing a local shopping mall, maintaining outdoor environmental quality, or creating indoor environmental comfort. But almost without exception, a consulting engineer can pursue his own interests and still touch the lives of many people around him.

As their name implies, consulting engineers are asked for advice, but that hardly suggests the imagination that goes into their work and the satisfaction that can be derived from this people-oriented profession.

Consulting engineers are called on when a prospective client with an engineering requirement (1) does not have expertise within his own organization to satisfy his need, (2) cannot free his engineering staff from present commitments, or (3) needs an outside, objective analysis.

Before undertaking the work, the consulting engineer normally signs a contract with the client and becomes, in effect, a temporary extension of the client's staff. When the client's need has been satisfied, the relationship usually ends. Frequently, however, a consulting engineer is employed on a continuing basis, for example, by local governmental agencies, to offer advice and provide engineering capability for ongoing client operations. Although such relations with one client may span months, years, or decades, the consulting engineer usually works simultaneously on a number of assignments for many clients.

Quality control begins early in the project. Contract negotiations with the client must be realistic, but they should be conducted in an atmosphere of understanding and mutual respect. Personnel assignments that do not overextend a firm's staff and a work schedule that allows sufficient time to be devoted to the assignment are essential in the early stages of a project.

Like a physician, attorney, or accountant, a consulting engineer practices a profession while at the same time operating a business. Although some professionals provide services primarily for individuals, consulting engineers more often provide professional services for corporations or public agencies. From a legal standpoint, there is a significant difference between consulting engineers and engineers employed by industry or government. The consulting engineer must be licensed to protect the public interest. While the engineer who works for an industry or government may be encouraged to become licensed, he works internally within an organization and his work does not necessarily affect the general public. The work of the consulting engineer, by contrast, involves the public welfare, and he is required by law to seal the plans and specifications that will result in the construction of such facilities as highways, water treatment plants, grain elevators, marinas, or nuclear power plants.

Because of the complex nature of the work, the newly graduated engineer seldom opens his own practice. The organization he joins as a young engineer may be individually owned, a partnership, or a corporation, and its size will vary accordingly. One individual and a part-time secretary may comprise an entire engineering staff, or a firm may include hundreds of employees in offices around the world. Just as the number of employees varies, so does the scope of work performed by any one firm.

Technical expertise in one firm may be limited to a narrow range of services, such as design of electrical components for buildings, provision of instrumentation control systems, structural engineering, or land surveying. Larger firms frequently offer a wide range of services in varied disciplines: civil, mechanical, electrical, water supply, treatment and distribution, sewage collection and treatment, electrical power generation, transmission and distribution, nuclear engineering, solar energy, gas, industrial, refuse collection and disposal, storm sewers, flood studies, dams, bridges, structures, tunnels, and community and regional planning. The staffs of such firms often include people trained and experienced in fields outside the engineering profession, such as city planning, architecture, economics, geology, archaeology, chemistry, physics, and graphic arts.

No matter how large an organization is, however, its staff rarely possesses all of the talent needed for every assignment. Since providing the best service for a client is essential for continuing progress, the consulting engineering firm must be aware of its limitations and know when to go outside the organization to obtain needed expertise. Total service may be provided through joint ventures or subcontracts on an interprofessional basis, or by utilizing outside individual experts. Interprofessional alliances may combine engineering firms or engineering and architectural firms. In fact, some consulting engineers—those in "interprofessional practice"—work exclusively for other engineers or architects.

Especially on large projects, joint ventures may be formed when two or more firms join to produce a third, temporary, organization. In legal terms, a joint venture is a new and taxable firm. In terms of the project, the client will work with the new firm rather than with two or more separate companies. By subcontracting, however, firms can form associations to serve a client without the formality of establishing a separate legal entity. Under a subcontracting arrangement, each firm retains its corporate identity, although the expertise needed for the project is pooled. Such arrangements can be fruitful when one company has the benefit of geographic location or a specifically needed capability. It may be to the client's advantage, though, for one firm to maintain prime responsibility to the client while another firm provides specialty services.

Studies and Reports

Frequently, a client will have a general idea of what he wants accomplished on a specific assignment, but he may be uncertain about the scope of work, the alternatives, or even the feasibility of the ultimate goal. This is how the consulting engineer begins many projects—by making studies and reports. Studies come in a variety of shapes and sizes, falling into the three general categories of planning studies, feasibility studies, and design studies. They may:

• Provide long-range planning

- Detail the scope of a project
- Investigate various alternatives
- Provide preliminary plans and cost estimates
- Determine potential financing arrangements
- Estimate future operation and maintenance and life-cycle costs
- Establish a project's feasibility in terms of both construction and economy
- Point out appropriate steps to implement the project
- Present the consultant's conclusions and recommendations

Planning studies have long been used by industry to determine new products, new markets, new plant sites, and future expansion. Such studies also are frequently used by municipalities and other governmental agencies as they establish policies on land use, transportation, sanitation, water supply, or power generation. A detailed study is required if, for instance, a municipal government considers whether it should buy the local, privately owned landing strip. The data may be largely demographic in nature, including details of both the work and living habits of local residents. This planning study would probably also include information about air carrier needs, as seen by commerce and industry experts, and describe services provided by nearby airfields. If the airfield has been newly purchased, a planning study would most likely include consideration of long-range, broadly described developments over the next 20 years or so. This would enable the new owners to plan their expansion while considering both the project's impact on community growth and its cost to the taxpayers.

Another type of study explores the feasibility of a given project. An idea may in itself be a good one, but it is necessary to determine whether it can be accomplished physically and at an economical cost to the client. For example, can polluted river water be cleansed acceptably so that it can be used as a drinking water supply? Questions that must be answered in this situation would include what types and quantities of pollutants are in the water; what is the state of the art with respect to removal of these pollutants; what methods of water treatment have been successful in the past; what equipment will be required; what are the Environmental Protection Agency (EPA) standards; and are the client standards more stringent? Feasibility studies and design studies may become linked during investigation of questions such as these, although design studies usually come later in the project sequence and are generally conducted in greater detail. It is important that the client contribute significantly to such investigations, especially in terms of specifying his needs, objectives, and existing conditions. Depending on the project, the study may involve specialty investigations such as soil borings, laboratory analyses, bench scale testing, pilot plant testing, and examination of similar existing installations.

Design studies are conducted to solve specific problems which either exist in the assignment or evolve during the feasibility studies. The amount of detail required in such a study will depend on the circumstances and often on the time limits imposed by the client. Since clients frequently are not entirely familiar with financing options, the consulting engineer should have knowledge of private, state, and federal funding sources and procedures to obtain financing from such sources, and he should be prepared to recommend the best option for the specific assignment. Additional information that becomes part of the study may require that the consulting engineer be aware of applicable codes, regulations, and possible regulation changes that could affect the overall project.

The Need to Communicate

Working with detailed study information, the consulting engineer comes to conclusions and recommendations that are included in a report submitted to the client and perhaps to various community groups and review agencies. The results of some studies may be reported to the client in a form as brief as a letter, but more typically, it is made in a bound volume. Presentation of reports such as these focuses on another important aspect of a consulting engineer's work, the ability to communicate clearly, both orally and on paper.

Since the consulting engineer is involved with projects that affect people, he cannot afford the luxury of too much technical jargon. Seldom is his audience made up strictly of engineers. More often, it is composed of lay persons who are not technically expert, and the results of the study must be understandable to such audiences as a corporate board of directors or a municipal governing body. Frequently, a project's needs require that a study report contain sufficient technical information for the client's technical staff and yet be written in language understandable to the lay person. If an oral presentation is required in conjunction with the written report, the use of photos, graphs, easily interpreted charts, and even slides can facilitate an understanding of the study's scope and conclusions. The consulting engineer's ability to communicate becomes even more crucial as the project enters the design phase.

Preliminary plans and specifications are to the total project what an outline is to a completed report. The preliminaries bring together initial design ideas, schematics, additional technical investigations if necessary, major materials, equipment, schedules, and preliminary cost estimates. At this stage it is still economical to make changes in the project design. As the project moves through the preliminary and detailed planning phases, drawings of the proposed concepts become increasingly important. Various types of drawings usually are involved in the same project. In the preliminary phase, those most often take the form of sketches that may be used to estimate a project's most basic needs in terms of equipment and space, but are not used for bidding or construction purposes. Since project drawings are the primary method of transmitting the ideas of a consulting engineer to contractors and suppliers, they must be prepared in an easily interpreted form.

Once the design is finalized into detailed plans and specifications, however, a change can become an expensive luxury. The need to make changes after construction has started is an even more serious situation and one to be avoided whenever possible. To avoid late changes, the consulting engineer must provide enough details in the plans and specifications to allow contractors to make intelligent estimates and prepare bids for construction. Design drawings graphically present a project's details. Should the client, contractor, and supplier be familiar with the type of design presented in the drawings, the amount of detail required may be somewhat less than would be necessary for an entirely new procedure. In addition to being technically accurate and easy to follow, design drawings also must be detailed enough to present all essential design information, and they must not differ from the written bidding requirements.

Shop drawings are furnished to the consulting engineer rather than by him. These drawings are prepared by manufacturers to show how the equipment they propose to furnish will fit into the overall project. For instance, in specifying that a motor starter is needed for a complex electrical project, the consulting engineer would receive from the manufacturer detailed drawings of the equipment including information on important details such as dimensions, capacity, and color. Review of shop drawings is essential to ensure that the plans and specification requirements of the consulting engineer have been interpreted correctly. Any changes suggested by the manufacturer must be reviewed with special care. Attention to this type of detail is part of the quality control expected from consulting engineers on each assignment.

During the design phase, consulting engineers are familiar enough with the sources, quality, service, and prices to detail the project's component items. Specifications add details for prospective bidders in terms of precise materials, construction processes, or standards for equipment needed for the current assignment. These specifications are the same for all bidders on the project. They must be clearly stated and yet technical enough to give a uniformly precise verbal picture of just what sizes, strengths, performances, or qualities a particular material or piece of equipment should have.

When the project is ready for bidding, the consulting engineer provides bidding information and contract documents for potential bidders. After bids are received, the consulting engineer analyzes the proposed prices and the qualifications of bidders. He then makes recommendations to the client regarding award of contracts. Although the relative costs set forth in the bids are vital, the prior performance and financial condition of the competing firms and the validity of the bids must also be considered. The consulting engineer recognizes that even though a bid price may be attractively low, this does not always assure that the bidder's performance will meet the standards expected by the client.

Setting up a proposed construction schedule also is of vital importance to the client. The consulting engineer will require the contractor to submit evidence that deliveries and installation will be sequenced to avoid costly delays and assure completion on time.

Quality Control

Throughout a project, quality control must be given the highest priority. Consulting engineers develop a reputation in this area so that potential clients recognize and seek out those firms with a successful history of quality control. As the assignment takes shape, checklists, reviews, and brainstorming sessions among personnel assigned to the project will help assure that the client is receiving the best service possible.

Value engineering is a form of quality control that has evolved fairly recently. Although the procedure has been used for some time on large federal projects, the value engineering approach did not expand to other areas much before the early 1970s. As with any project evaluation, value engineering considers such areas as materials, capital costs, and operating costs. It differs from a routine project evaluation in that it is a formalized, multidisciplined process that generally involves about five people over a week's time.

For instance, in consideration of a proposed wastewater treatment facility, a value engineering review team might include an environmental engineer, a structural engineer, an electrical engineer, and a contractor. Usually only one of the team has had previous contact with the project. The earliest point for such a review probably would be during the preliminary design stage. Another value engineering review might be made when construction plans are 80 percent completed. Obviously, many projects are not of sufficient magnitude to tie up the required manpower for the time needed to complete a value engineering review. Many firms, however, use a modified value engineering approach in review of their design plans.

Attention to quality control during the design and bidding stages could be wasted if adequate inspection by the consulting engineer is not carried out during construction. The scope of this inspection is spelled out in the engineering agreement for each assignment. Many forms of inspection are rather general in nature, such as review of partial payment requests or checking schedules to be sure deliveries are made on time. Materials testing may be done both at the jobsite and in the office or lab. On-site inspections assure that the design is translated into a completed project that performs as it was intended. Progress reports and even photographic records during construction are of benefit not only to the client but also for future reference should a legal problem develop. On larger projects, the consulting engineer furnishes a resident engineer and inspectors throughout the construction process. In some instances, adequate contact may be provided without full-time on-the-job inspection.

A clear distinction exists between those construction services furnished by consulting engineers and those furnished by the contractor. The contractor's superintendent or foreman directs workers on the project and is responsible for safety. The contractor's representative "supervises" the work. On the other hand, the consulting engineer makes certain that the contractor has correctly interpreted the plans and specifications and that the desired quality is obtained. With the possible exception of a breach of safety standards that could result in an immediate danger to life or property, the consulting engineer will not take direct action with any worker. He deals exclusively with the contractor's representative or the owner.

The resident engineer works at a construction site to assure that the project design is correctly interpreted by contractors. Depending on the size of the project, he may have a staff of several additional engineers and technicians overseeing separate project components. For instance, on a large highway project the staff might include a pavement inspector, bridge inspector, asphalt inspector, and materials inspector.

As construction proceeds, new conditions not anticipated when plans were prepared often require changes in the work that may affect the cost of the project or the time of completion. The consulting engineer reviews the need for changes and, if appropriate, prepares "change order" forms for approval by the client. The change orders, when approved by the client and the contractor, become amendments to the construction contract. The consulting engineer also plays an important role in the final inspection prior to acceptance of the project by the owner.

Depending on the type of project, operation and maintenance manuals, which are detailed and frequently lengthy, are prepared by the consulting engineer for the client as the project nears completion. Such manuals include operating procedures, maintenance schedules, manufacturers' literature, replacement sources, and names and addresses of servicing firms which may be needed during the life of the project.

Even when construction is completed, the work of the consulting engineer may continue. He is often actively involved in start-up operations at the site, which may include supervision of initial equipment testing, training of equipment operators, supervision of start-up, or even the actual initial operation of the equipment.

As-built drawings are provided for the client as an important future reference tool. These drawings may differ slightly from the earlier completed plans and specifications, including any changes made in the field as a result of material substitutions or change orders. Indeed, some follow-up details may persist even after the client has taken over the project. Questions about operations, equipment problems, or minor adjustments may arise, and the consulting engineer must give these his attention. Clients remember the extra services they receive.

Yet another type of service which some firms provide is termed "construction management" or "contract management." Under such arrangements, the consulting engineering firm takes over many duties usually performed by a general contractor on a particular assignment. It then becomes the responsibility of the engineering firm to direct project construction. This might involve provision of detailed work schedules and periodic schedule updates, ordering of major equipment, selection of contractors and contract negotiations between contractors and project owners, project inspection, acceptance or rejection of completed work phases, coordination of various phases of work, approval of suppliers' and contractors' payment requests, and preparation of as-built record drawings.

In some areas of the construction industry, the consulting engineer finds himself in competition with "design-build" or "turnkey" firms that offer complete services from the initial study phase to completion. The consulting engineer nonetheless believes that because he acts as the owner's agent in designing the project and inspecting its construction, he can assure that the owner's interests are met and produce a better quality of work.

Other Consulting Services

Although consulting engineers must not infringe upon the practice of other professionals, they must be sufficiently familiar with the work of others to know when outside counsel is needed. A working knowledge of laws, regulations, accounting principles, fiscal affairs, and their effect on engineering practice and the clients' welfare are absolutely essential. As a professional in his own right, the consulting engineer sometimes is called upon to provide expert testimony in trials or hearings. Such occasions include, but are certainly not limited to, contract disputes, instances of machinery failure, accidents, or right-of-way disputes. Although such testimony may be given informally to a lawyer for a particular client, the consulting engineer must be prepared to provide expert testimony in court. In this case, the attorney is made totally familiar with the testimony that the engineer will present. The engineer should be ready to present his information with any visual charts, pictures, mechanical models, or other aids that will help laymen understand exactly what he is saying. Although distinctions must be made between fact and opinion during such testimony, the consulting engineer is permitted to offer his professional opinion in his role as an expert.

Yet another type of challenge for consulting engineers lies in the international arena. The benefits of updated and changing technology are being requested by many nations, and international practice often serves the national interest as well. When designs call for U.S.-made products, satisfactory performance of those products will perpetuate contact with the U.S. firms and enhance the United States' balance of trade. International practice is similar in many respects to the requirements of domestic clients. Studies are needed; plans, specifications, and construction inspection are all basically the same. However, the entire assignment is flavored by its international basis. Underdeveloped countries often require that consulting engineers utilize local nationals to a maximum extent in order that they may receive training. Some such countries insist on participation of local engineers in ownership of the engineering organization providing the services.

The availability of staff personnel for overseas assignments, the need for instruction in the host language and customs, the stability of the host government and its currency, the availability of qualified personnel to operate the proposed facility, the availability of materials, and tax and legal requirements that might affect payment must be studied when considering overseas work. An additional challenge of overseas assignments is the realization that solutions that might be standard on a domestic project may not work overseas. Climatic conditions, the availability of resources and aptitude for training of personnel, and the availability of repair services and parts may mean that a standard design cannot be used.

Depending on the location, size, and complexity of the assignment, the consulting engineer may work in one of several capacities. A recent graduate may be initially assigned as a staff engineer, working as an assistant to a design engineer or to a resident engineer on construction. With increased experience, he will be given design functions to perform, along with the title of design engineer. Once he becomes registered, he is permitted to seal plans, and he may then attain the position of project engineer on particular assignments. The project engineer correlates information from the client and project manager and oversees the project design team. The project manager is designated to supervise the entire assignment and act as liaison between the client and other subcontracted engineers or architects. Regardless of what his job might be, the consulting engineer must realize that he not only is demonstrating his own ideas and competence, but is affecting the reputation of his firm on every assignment he undertakes.

Since there usually are several firms well qualified for any particular job, consulting engineers do compete with each other and at times with public agencies, research foundations, and "package deal" or design-build organizations. Competition among consulting engineers is normally on the basis of qualification and experience rather than on the basis of price. Most firms soon learn that the best advertisement is a satisfied client, who in turn becomes the best prospect for a repeat engagement. Nonetheless, many firms have developed organized marketing efforts within the company. While maintaining contacts with former clients, initiating new contacts, and keeping an eye out for potential new jobs, they seek to sell the firm's competent services in a professional manner and without any of the Madison Avenue ballyhoo usually associated with selling.

Just as there are professional ethics associated with securing a client, there are also ethical standards involved in providing services during the performance of the project. One of the principal responsibilities is maintaining the client's confidentiality. During many assignments, the consulting engineer becomes a virtual extension of the client's company or office. In developing the studies and plans for the project, he can become privy to much information about the client's operations that must be kept confidential. Revealing privileged information about a client's affairs, copying the plans developed for a previous client at a later time, or taking advantage of a client's information for personal gain are sure ways to lose the respect of the client and possibly create legal difficulties as well. It is equally important that the consulting engineer maintain his independence and objectivity. He must avoid any conflict of interest that might impede his impartiality in his relations with contractors or with manufacturers of products that his client might use. Should such conflicts develop in the course of an assignment, the client should be informed immediately.

In times such as these, with change occurring at an increasingly rapid rate and with the horizons of technological progress constantly growing broader, it is essential that the consulting engineer continue to function independent of any special interest. The profession has never been more stimulating or its prospects more rewarding, and the consulting engineer must stand ready to meet the challenge.

Chapter 2

MAJOR ENGINEERING DISCIPLINES

Thomas B. Robinson

Managing Partner, Black & Veatch, Consulting Engineers

A Brief History

The history of engineering is an essential part of the record of civilization. Through the ages, the engineer has stood, along with the scientist, at the point of contact between human needs and the world's resources. Scientists and engineers have long been partners. The engineer, with a background of scientific knowledge, has put this knowledge to work in behalf of such vital elements of civilization as water supply, energy, agriculture, and transportation. Engineering is, as it always has been, the efficient utilization of the materials and forces of nature for the benefit of humanity (Cross, 1952; Florman, 1976).

Sprague de Camp, in his scholarly account of ancient engineering practices (de Camp, 1974), tells us that the story of civilization is the story of engineering and also that this story, "pieced together from dusty manuscripts and crumbling relics, explains as well the state of the world today as all the accounts of kings and philosophers, generals and politicians." The work of the ancient engineers often included important water supply and architectural projects, as well as military facilities such as forts and water towers. Engineering specialties had not yet developed. Anyone recognized as an engineer was expected to practice in many fields.

The water supply of the city of Rome was a notable, ancient engineering achievement and its story was recorded by Sextus Julius Frontinus (1973) who was appointed *curator-aquarum* (water commissioner) for Rome in A.D. 97. We are indebted to Clemens Herschel, a distinguished American engineer, for the translation of the Frontinus book. The result is a classic account of ancient engineering. Unfortunately, many of the records of ancient engineering practice have been lost, and much of the history of engineering must be gleaned from structures that have survived. Some works of impressive proportions have endured for centuries in the orient, the middle east, and Europe, and also in the western hemisphere. The Inca civilization flourished until the sixteenth century in South America, and the Incas are said to have "excelled as engineers" (Thorndike, 1979). Surviving buildings and roads confirm this.

Engineering in America

In the United States, the need for engineers became critical during the Revolutionary War. Congress authorized an engineer corps in 1776, but there were few experienced engineers available for duty with the American forces. General Washington had to appeal to France for engineering assistance. After the war, the need for engineers continued, and an early step toward meeting the shortage was the establishment of the U. S. Military Academy at West Point, New York. Its mission included instruction in the principles of engineering. In 1821, the Congress directed that surveys be made of certain roads and canals under the direction of "engineer officers" and "civil engineers" (Wisely, 1974). This is believed to be the earliest official notice of the developing distinction between military and civilian or "civil" engineering activities. Further recognition came in 1823 when a course entitled "civil engineering," which dealt with bridges, roads, and canals, was offered at the West Point academy.

The Academy furnished most of the academically trained engineers during the years 1800–1850, but could not supply the needs of a constantly expanding nation. As a consequence, many engineers who practiced in the 1800s had little formal technical education. Their technical knowledge was acquired principally through self-study and apprenticeship. The road, canal, and railroad projects with which they were involved served as their classrooms and laboratories; the "faculty" was composed of older, more experienced engineers. The first civil engineering degree was conferred by Rensselaer Polytechnic Institute in 1835. By about 1870, some 75 schools offered engineering programs. The nineteenth century saw the beginning of a golden age of change, growth, and challenge for engineers and engineering. Professional status was established in Britain by the formation of the British Institution of Civil Engineers in 1818. By about 1850, national engineering organizations had been formed in Holland, Belgium, Germany, and France, and there was clear need for similar organizations in America.

Organizational efforts began in the United States about 1836. Among the early local engineering organizations was the Boston Society of Civil Engineers, still an active organization, which was formed in 1848. The first national organization was the American Society of Civil Engineers (ASCE), established in 1852. Membership was about 200 in 1870 and 2000 in 1900. Current membership is approximately 75,000. The society has been a significant force in engineering education and practice in America for well over 100 years (Hoy, 1976).

Growth and Evolution

Engineering can hardly be defined within easy limits. Along with the growth of the profession, there has been change, and the last century has seen the development of several major engineering branches or disciplines and numerous areas of specialization within these disciplines. Civil engineering, the oldest discipline, by tradition includes the design and construction of structures of widely varying sizes and functions—dams, bridges, railroads, highways, airports, pipelines, canals, buildings of many kinds, levees, works for water supply and wastewater treatment and disposal, power plants, storm drains, and shipyards and docks. Because of its broad scope and complexity, it is not surprising that from civil engineering many specialized areas of engineering practice have evolved. Some of the prominent specialties closely identified with civil engineering are structural engineering, surveying, construction management, soil mechanics, hydraulics, mining, environmental engineering, highway engineering, public works engineering, and railroad engineering. Civil engineers find employment in private practice as general and specialized consultants; with federal, state, county, and municipal agencies; in construction; in industry; and in education.

Energy—its generation, distribution, and utilization—is the essence of engineering. Ancient engineers wrestled with energy problems and developed methods to supplement human and animal effort through the use of mechanical devices powered by wind and water. During the early nineteenth century, there was a critical need for engineers who possessed an interest in machinery and a competence in machine and steam engine design. The need was met by the development of the broad field of mechanical engineering, a major branch of the engineering profession. National organizations of mechanical engineers were formed in Britain in 1847 and in 1880 in the United States. The current membership of the American Society of Mechanical Engineers (ASME) numbers approximately 80,000.

Today's mechanical engineers are challenged by the need to use existing energy sources more efficiently and to assist in the development of new sources, including solar, nuclear, and synthetic fuel. The design of efficient systems for energy generation, transmission, and utilization—plus a multiplicity of mechanical devices ranging from pumps and machine tools to space exploration equipment—is the province of the mechanical engineer. Mechanical engineering specialties include nuclear and industrial engineering and the design of systems for heating, ventilating, and air conditioning.

Electrical engineering has influenced virtually every facet of human activity within a century. This branch of engineering deals with the practical everyday applications of electrical energy and magnetism. Familiar examples are lighting, a host of home appliances, and automotive ignition systems. The closely related engineering field of electronics has made possible the present high state of development of telephone systems, radio, radar, television, computers, medical electronics, and control systems. In addition to electronics, electrical engineering specialties include power generation, electrical machinery, and illumination. Early advances in electrical engineering were associated with nineteenth-century discoveries by Henry, Faraday, Morse, Edison, Bell, Tesla, Hertz, Gibbs, and others. The development of electrical engineering began and moved rapidly ahead during the latter half of the last century. To meet the needs of the growing profession, the American Institute of Electrical Engineers (AIEE) was formed in 1884, and the Institute of Radio Engineers (IRE) in 1913. These organizations eventually merged and became the Institute of Electrical and Electronics Engineers (IEEE) whose present membership of approximately 200,000 makes it the largest of the engineering organizations.

Chemical engineering, the newest of the four major engineering disciplines, serves mankind principally through the application and control of chemical processes. Chemical reactions and the principles that influence them play major roles in vital life processes, important industries, and the environment. Chemistry and chemical engineering touch nearly every aspect of human activity. Chemical conversions are involved in the production of such things as magnesium and bromine from sea water, paper from wood, and gasoline from petroleum. Synthetic fibers, drugs, antibiotics, and fertilizers are manufactured by processes developed and controlled by chemical engineers, whose knowledge of chemical and biochemical processes, reaction kinetics, and properties of materials, as well as engineering fundamentals, enables them to contribute to the solution of environmental problems. Many chemical engineers find professional employment as air-pollution-control specialists and in the fields of water and industrial waste treatment and disposal. Chemical engineers also have long played a prominent role in energy-related industries involving coal, oil, and gas, and have made important contributions to the development of nuclear energy. Early chemical engineering in America was influenced by German, British, and French practice, but currently the United States stands high among the world leaders in chemical engineering. The American Institute of Chemical Engineers was formed in 1908, and current membership is approximately 40,000.

Civil Engineering

Consulting civil engineering is so multifaceted and all-encompassing that it becomes rather difficult to define accurately. In 1963, *Engineering News-Record* (*ENR*) asked civil engineering department heads at 32 universities to define civil engineering ("What's Going on in CE Education"). *ENR* sorted out only one answer it believed to be acceptable: "The engineering of systems of constructed facilities." The generalities and the variable nature inherent in the practice of civil engineering are certainly implicit in this definition. A more comprehensive definition appeared in a subsequent *ENR* editorial entitled "Civil Engineering Needs Definition":

Engineering is the application of laws of science, mathematics, and economics for the production of things. And civil engineering is the principal branch of engineering concerned with things constructed as opposed to things manufactured, mined, grown, or generated. (p. 26)

The key words are "concerned with things constructed." This concern is paramount in the entire process of conception, planning, design, and building of any project.

Related Specialties

Variety is intrinsic to the activities of the civil engineer in private practice. It is this variety that makes this field of endeavor so alluring to professional engineers of all ages and levels of experience. To some extent, the engineering specialties listed by the National Society of Professional Engineering as related to civil engineering display the variety of activities in which the civil engineer is involved:

Agriculture
Airports
Appraisals
Architecture
Beach erosion
Bridges
Channels, rivers, canals,
  waterways
Cost consulting
Dams
Dredging
Environmental assessment
Flood control
Foundations
Highways
Hydraulics
Hydrology
Irrigation
Landscape architecture
Marine structures
Mining
Natural resources surveys

Navigation locks
Oceanography
Parking facilities
Photogrammetry
Pipelines
Planning
Port facilities
Pumping stations
Railroads, rapid transit
Rate studies
Reclamation
Sewage and wastewater collection,
  treatment, and disposal
Soil and rock mechanics
Solid waste disposal
Storm sewers
Structures
Surveying and mapping
Transportation and traffic studies
Tunnels
Water supply treatment, storage,
  and distribution

All of these specialties involve things constructed in some manner. In fact, some of those listed are basic building blocks for other specialties. These building blocks would include structures, soil and rock mechanics, engineering mechanics, hydraulics, and surveying and mapping. One or more of these building blocks are generally associated with specialized knowledge to create a specialty field in civil engineering. For example, water supply, treatment, storage, and distribution would include essentially all of the building blocks plus the specialized knowledge of processes for treatment of water. Similarly, pumping stations would include structures, soil and rock mechanics, and hydraulics, along with specialized knowledge concerning pumps, motors, and ancillary equipment.

In addition to these specialties, civil engineering is interrelated with all of the other major engineering disciplines, and so the accomplished consultant must acquire knowledge and experience in those disciplines as well as his own. On many multidisciplined projects, the civil engineer coordinates the efforts of all the engineering groups, including electrical, mechanical, chemical, and various other types of engineers, to ensure proper completion of the project. The use of the full range of building blocks, plus specialized knowledge in many other related areas, provides the civil engineer with a broad base of knowledge and experience.

Opportunities

A variety of assignments, duties, and career paths awaits the aspiring civil engineering graduate in a consulting firm. He may be involved in any of the following work areas:

Preliminary conceptual study of the facility to be constructed to determine the optimum size, nature, and type of components

Rate, financial and economic studies, value engineering, and other management services

Final design, including calculations, the preparation of plans, materials and equipment specifications, and contract documents

Review of equipment and materials proposed by the contractor, or assisting with on-site inspection during construction

Assistance with operation of the completed facility

This is, of course, an incomplete listing, but it indicates the diversity of activity open to civil engineers. As the young engineer gains experience and expertise, his level of involvement and responsibility also increases.

Civil engineers in the consulting field have the opportunity not only to work on a variety of projects but also to work on both a large and small scale. For example, a civil engineer could design anchor bolts on one phase of a project and shortly thereafter be involved in the layout of a large airport or wastewater treatment plant. The ability of the civil engineer to work on projects of such different scales creates interest in the work and provides a perspective for both the pieces of a project and the project as a whole.

Civil engineers have an opportunity to broaden their knowledge and experience with each assignment in a consulting firm. No two assignments will be exactly the same, and the opportunity for learning is available with each new task. The opportunity can either broaden the civil engineer's capabilities into other specialty areas or deepen his expertise within a particular specialty. In addition, some of the learning experience will include development in other engineering disciplines and even in nonengineering fields such as economics and law.

Specialist versus Generalist

As a consulting civil engineer's career unfolds, he must decide, at some juncture, whether he wishes to be a generalist or a specialist. Some choose to concentrate on only one of the aspects of civil engineering and become specialists. These individuals advance in their engineering firms on the basis of their ability to do the work involved in only certain aspects of a project, such as structures or environmental processes. Other civil engineers choose to remain involved in most or all of the aspects of civil engineering and serve as generalists, although this does not preclude their becoming experts in a specialized area.

People typically advance in their consulting firms to project management positions on the basis of their leadership, performance, and overall knowledge of project development. Management responsibilities begin with supervising and coordinating the work of others and progress to the administration of a project to provide the engineering services required by the client within budget and time restraints. Finally, a consulting civil engineer can reach the level of management and administration at which he is totally responsible for the execution of a particular project. And for some, the management and administrative role develops into the leadership of a consulting engineering firm.

The choice between generalist and specialist must be based on one's own capabilities, goals, and preferences, but either choice can lead to a rewarding and challenging career.

Structural Engineering

One of the major areas of concentration in which civil engineers specialize is structural engineering. "Civil-structurals," as they are often referred to, generally are graduated as civil engineers with a concentration of course work in structural engineering. There are a few universities, however, that provide degrees in structural engineering as a separate discipline.

Consulting firms provide graduating structural engineers with a wide range of employment opportunities. There are small (2- to 10-person) consulting firms which specialize in structures, and perhaps further specialize in designing structures of a particular material, such as precast, prestressed concrete. At the other end of the spectrum are large, multidiscipline consulting firms (100 or more engineers) designing major projects.

Consulting firms offer the structural engineer an opportunity to design a variety of structures, such as a multilevel office parking complex, a large industrial facility, an electric-power-generating station, or a stadium or arena. The structure designed for an office building may tower a hundred stories above the earth's surface, while the structure designed for a water-pumping station or national defense installation may extend several stories underground.

The structural engineer challenges the elements of nature in his work. Typhoons, hurricanes, tornadoes, thunderstorms, rain, snow, ice, earthquakes, even soil and rock will push, pull, and shake the structure he has designed. In addition, the structural engineer must recognize the loads and forces of humanity—people, automobiles, machinery, and other types of human necessities and conveniences —that are placed in, on, and next to structures; he must design each structure to withstand these forces, and he must do so at the most economical cost.

The basic materials used in the design of structures have not changed over the years; however, the shapes and applications have changed constantly, as economics demand more efficient utilization of these materials. In his design work, the structural engineer uses tools that can range from a pocket calculator to a sophisticated, high-speed computer.

In response to the complex performance requirements of the nuclear power industry, structural engineers are continually enhancing the state of the art, which in turn benefits other design endeavors. In the earthquake engineering field, computer programs have been developed which consider the responses of the complete power plant with its multiplicity of structural, mechanical, and electrical components. Interactions of the soil with the structures and fluid "sloshing" effects are considered, and, in certain cases, the inelastic behavior is studied. The structural analyst uses his expertise to predict the dynamic response of structures and equipment to shock loading from postulated accident conditions or tornado-borne missiles, as well as to answer architects' and designers' questions about the behavior of structures in response to large temperature excursions. These are just a few of the many challenges awaiting graduating structural engineers who choose to enter private practice.

The work of the structural engineer is the important aspect of the overall project; his work supports and holds together the efforts of the other engineering disciplines. It is the structural engineer's contribution that defines each structure's form and function, which constitute an integral part of its beauty. The structural engineer can derive much satisfaction in realizing the trust people place in his knowledge and professional ability every time they enter a building or cross a bridge.

Mechanical Engineering

Careful investigation of the career opportunities available to a mechanical engineer will soon prove that the possibilities are nearly limitless. For example, the young graduate in mechanical engineering can consider aerospace, applied mechanics, materials handling, diesel or gas engine power, fuels, safety, fluids engineering, bioengineering, materials, heat transfer, process industries, production engineering, design engineering, lubrication, petroleum, nuclear engineering, rail transportation, power, and textile industries.

Other areas in which he may concentrate are plant engineering and maintenance, gas turbines, air pollution control, dynamic system design and control, ocean engineering, energetics, pressure vessels and piping, solid waste processing, solar energy, computer engineering, and noise control and abatement.

The graduating mechanical engineer must choose an area of mechanical engineering in which to begin his career and concentrate his efforts.

Career Selection

When most graduating engineers recall why they made engineering their career choice, they usually discover that their motivations have not changed much since they were freshmen. The same is true of the personal interests that influence those who have selected mechanical engineering as a career. Like other members of the engineering profession, the successful mechanical engineer has to have that personal drive to create, design, and build a new way of accomplishing an end result or of improving an existing concept.

With the broad range of career possibilities available in mechanical engineering, it is possible to overlook the opportunity for a career which has the potential of interacting with virtually all facets of mechanical engineering as well as the other engineering disciplines —a career as a mechanical engineer in a consulting engineering practice.

Project Team

The young mechanical engineer joining a consulting engineering firm is brought into close association with professional mechanical engineers assigned to a project team which prepares the engineering design and construction plans for a specific project. Such a project could be a large multiunit electric generating station, an expansive industrial or manufacturing plant, a commercial building development, a multiuse government facility, or a solar energy test facility. In this environment, he is challenged to apply his acquired skills and knowledge in applied thermodynamics, heat transfer, fluid flow, kinematics and dynamics of machines, machine design, engineering economics, and other fundamentals of mechanical engineering to solve real problems.

As a member of a project team, he would assist in the activities of preparing conceptual design studies or feasibility analyses for the mechanical systems required by the project. As an example, large steam and electric power-generating plant projects typically have between 50 and 60 mechanical systems to be investigated. Based on the results of these studies and analyses, decisions are made which allow the project team to develop detailed engineering design and construction plans.

First Assignments

During the detailed engineering phase of a project, the mechanical engineer is involved in establishing system design parameters, control philosophy, equipment characteristics, and component attributes required to satisfy the operating conditions of the system under design. He could possibly be associated with the development of technical specifications or bills of material for the purchase of the mechanical equipment and components. Preparation of technical specifications or bills of material requires an extended knowledge and experience combined with good written communication skills, which allow the mechanical engineer to express in clear, concise terms the equipment or component requirements.

Another area in which the mechanical engineer frequently takes part is the preparation of cost estimates. Estimating requires a knowledge of ways and means, an appreciation of the contingencies which may be encountered, and a knowledge of labor and material costs and transportation and construction charges.

When the engineering design and construction plans are completed, equipment and components are purchased, and contracts for the performance of the work of construction are awarded, the young mechanical engineer's duties are not finished. Assigned as a member of the project construction management team, he inspects the work to determine that it has been performed in accordance with the engineering design specifications and construction plans. Here the mechanical engineer becomes an arbiter in deciding upon the meaning and intent of the plans and in interpreting the specifications.

Career Growth

As he advances in his career, the mechanical engineer will come in contact with engineers of other disciplines, manufacturers and contractors, officials of private or public corporations, clients, lawyers, investors, bankers, interveners, and a great variety of other persons having various interests. He will be responsible for all mechanical engineering work associated with a specific project, requiring that he provide direct supervision of other mechanical engineers and technical support personnel.

As experience, judgment, and broader knowledge are acquired, the mechanical engineer may be called upon to manage a large multidiscipline project of great complexity, such as a large refinery or steel plant. In a project of this scope, he may be responsible not only for the project's engineering design, but also for planning, feasibility and cost studies, construction management, and ongoing operational assistance. The legal requirements under state and federal laws must be considered, associated hazards and contingencies must be clearly understood, and possible methods and expenses of financing must be known. No element that goes to make the project a complete commercial success can be neglected if the consulting engineering firm which employs him is to retain its clientele and reputation.

In the diversified work of a consulting engineering firm, the mechanical engineer may appear before councils, legislatures, boards of directors, stockholders, bankers, and investors to explain in nonengineering terms the scope, cost, and benefits of an engineering project. He also may be called before the court to give expert testimony and evidence in engineering matters. Here, experience, judgment, knowledge, reputation, and communication skills are of great importance.

An Important Role

The role of a mechanical engineer in consulting engineering practice is varied and challenging. He formulates ideas and develops them into a reality by investigating conditions and determining the best methods by which those conditions can be used or modified to obtain the required results. In the role of supervisor, he must plan the activities and determine the resources required to accomplish the assigned work on schedule and within budget. He directs and guides the work of other mechanical engineers and technical support personnel and instructs them by example in the methods and procedures to use in performing assignments. In addition, he checks the work as it develops to ensure that a high standard of quality is maintained.

As a manager, the consulting engineer soon loses his limited perspective as a mechanical engineer and develops a broad overview, not only of technical knowledge, but also of finance, economics, business methods, and legal relations. To fulfill these various roles and functions is an exciting challenge for young mechanical engineers in the consulting field.

Electrical Engineering

The student electrical engineer approaching graduation is eager to find employment that is meaningful. Although there are many areas that satisfy this desire, none will do it better than the field of consulting engineering.

As a member of a consulting organization, the newly graduated electrical engineer will be provided with work assignments and possibly with formal training. However, most education, which must continue for a lifetime, will be provided by on-the-job experience. This results from the frequent need for study and research to solve the problems inherent in each work assignment. As he gains experience, the engineer can improve his expertise in the technical field and attain recognition as an authority or accept opportunities for advancement into management. However, the work itself is inherently satisfying because the engineer is able to see the project develop from start to finish and to be involved in its design.

Consulting work offers the opportunity, possibly more than any other field of engineering work, to become part of management while continuing to perform as an engineer. Supervision of the work of a few drafters and technicians is the first step in management. Except for technical support and administrative areas, management throughout the organization, to the very top, is composed of engineers.

The opportunities for the electrical engineer become apparent when one considers the types of consulting services performed and the variety of clients served: electrical utilities; petroleum, natural gas, and chemical companies; military and related organizations; water supply and sewage disposal utilities; and commercial and institutional organizations.

Electrical Utilities

Of the many services provided by consulting engineers to electrical utilities, the most extensive are assignments involving the design of electricity-generating facilities. A large generating unit addition, for example, may cost over a billion dollars and involve a design staff of 250 employees. Of this group, approximately 25 percent are electrical and control personnel.

The electrical power engineer is involved in two general areas: (1) getting the plant's product (electricity) into the electrical system, and (2) providing motors, and power to operate the motors, for driving numerous mechanical devices such as pumps, compressors, blowers, and crushers. This involves the design of the plant's electrical power system, which requires between 5 and 10 percent of the generator's capacity. Some of the equipment typically furnished by numerous volumes of Electrical Purchase and Construction specifications for a large coal-fired generating unit (750 megawatts) may include 2500 motors, heaters, and panelboards; eighty 6900-volt power circuit breakers; 2500 miles of conductor; 80 miles of conduit

(¾- to 4-inch diameter); 5 miles of cable tray (6- to 36-inch width); and 5100 lighting fixtures.

The control engineers, many of whom are electrical engineers, provide for the safe, reliable, and functional integration of components within each system and between systems. This is partially accomplished through interfacing control computers and programmable controllers. It also involves the integration of power plant information for the control and protection of the equipment.

Of the numerous illustrations that might be selected, two give a glimpse of the importance of the control engineer: (1) in the event of emergencies such as the loss of all generator load or the loss of the boiler fans, the entire unit must be automatically tripped immediately; or (2) if a coal belt is stopped for any reason, all equipment feeding coal to the belt must be stopped immediately.

The control engineer also is responsible for designing the combustion-control equipment so that a minimum of fuel is required. This must be done automatically under changing load conditions. To accomplish these responsibilities, the control engineer applies the necessary instrumentation, monitoring, and control equipment, which may involve computers and programmable controllers and may include the development of much of the software requirements. In the performance of these responsibilities, the control engineers on a large generating unit will produce hundreds of logic, schematic, and interconnection diagrams.

The electrical design work involves developing specifications of the electrical equipment for procurement and preparing a comprehensive set of construction plans and specifications for use by the electrical contractor selected to erect the equipment and interconnect it. Some of the design and all of the graphic assignments are performed by technicians and drafters under the direction of the electrical engineers. This frees the engineers to perform the studies necessary to facilitate their selection of equipment and systems and to coordinate and manage the efforts of all electrical personnel on the project.

Occasionally, when exceptional growth occurs, the engineering staff of some electric utilities becomes overloaded. For this reason, many consulting engineers provide additional services to utilities, typically in the areas of transmission, substations management, distribution, communications, protective relaying, and power system dispatching facilities.

Although most engineering is concerned with design, many assignments originate with a study. Electrical engineers prepare studies as needed on such items as load flow, faults, system stability, protective relay application, relay settings, voltage selection, facility location, and size. The computer is employed extensively for study projects.

The responsibilities of the electrical engineer performing in a consulting capacity for the electrical utility industry are representative of the responsibilities of the consulting electrical engineer in general because the objectives and procedures are similar for services provided to other organizations. All types of electrical work in the consulting engineering field are challenging because of the diversity of assignments coming from a variety of clients.

Petroleum, Natural Gas, and Chemical Companies

A large organization with a number of disciplines, including electrical engineers, is required in such activities as the design of a refinery or chemical complex. Although the product created is different, the design of such large facilities is similar to the design of electric generating stations in many ways. Sometimes steam or electric generation, possibly by cogeneration, is involved. The organization and procedures, particularly in relation to the electrical engineering work, are parallel to that of power plant design.

The transport of natural gas and, to some extent, petroleum as a raw product or in its finished state, often is by underground pipeline. The consulting engineer's services are frequently needed when new lines are to be built. Compressor or pumping stations located at intervals along the line are required, and it is in these areas that the expertise of the electrical engineer is needed. When natural gas is liquefied, primarily for storage and peaking, his services also are required.

Military and Related Organizations

Numerous types of facilities are required by U.S. military organizations in which electrical engineers provide both studies and design for such items as power supplies (including electric generation and cogeneration), energy conservation, manufacturing facilities and

laboratories for munitions, explosives test facilities, aircraft navigation aids, and security systems. Similar services are sometimes supplied to foreign governments, particularly their military branches,
through the encouragement of our own government as an extension
of its diplomacy. Corporate manufacturers of munitions and military electronic gear also employ consulting engineers.

In addition to substations and generation facilities, the electrical
engineer is involved in numerous other areas, such as communications, security, lighting and surveillance, remote control, and auto-
mated data acquisition systems. The objectives in some of these
areas are accomplished by the utilization of closed circuit television,
remote handling equipment, microprocessors, and remote radio control.

Water Supply and Sewage Disposal Utilities

Some water systems, particularly those associated with the larger
cities, require electrical engineering in connection with furnishing
and controlling power drives for pumps, air compressors, heaters,
scrapers, conveyors, and traveling screens. Electrical engineering
also may be required in providing centralized control and supervision to improve the operation of a water system, and to minimize
power costs and the number of operating personnel.

In sewage collection and processing, the electrical engineer is
primarily involved with motors to drive pumps and the associated
control, and is similarly concerned with many of the same types of
equipment employed for the public water supply systems. Storm
drainage systems also principally involve motor-driven pumps.

Lighting is required in all of these facilities. Often remote supervisory control is specified to properly follow changing flows and to
alternate pump and motor usage with the detailed requirements set
forth by the electrical engineer.

Commercial and Institutional Organizations

Even though the design of large buildings is the architect's domain,
more than half of the design work is performed by engineers. Numerous consulting engineering firms offer services in connection
with and for architectural firms that include the design of electric

power systems for public and commercial buildings. Such systems encompass heating, ventilating, and air conditioning; elevators and electric stairways; lighting; building safety and security systems; and the associated centralized monitoring and control facilities.

Chemical Engineering

All things in our world relate to chemistry—some to a major extent, such as the human body, the most complex chemical plant ever created, and some, such as a filter for a household water faucet, to a much lesser extent. The chemical engineer utilizes his knowledge of chemistry, along with his broad knowledge of engineering principles, to further civilization's progress, and his expertise is an essential part of many major engineering efforts today.

The chemical engineer has demonstrated significant value to the profession of consulting engineering. The understanding and proper application of chemical engineering principles, such as those related to corrosion control, chemical handling, membrane and ion-exchange processes, and environmental considerations, contribute to the success of many modern projects.

New challenges are presented daily to the chemical engineer in the consulting field, providing him the opportunity to expand his technical knowledge and professional development. Projects typically grow in size and complexity as progress is made, and the chemical engineer finds new interest in his work as the application of previously satisfactory solutions may be found no longer adequate or appropriate.

For example, chemical engineering work with a consulting firm could involve participation in the design of a multimillion-dollar industrial complex. On such a project, the chemical engineer will be part of a large multidiscipline team dealing with many people in various working relationships—other chemical engineers, as well as civil, electrical, and mechanical engineers. He also will coordinate the project with the client's management and engineering staffs and maintain relations with regulatory authorities and the public.

Specific areas in power generation in which the chemical engineer with a consulting firm may become involved include water supply and treatment, water reuse, waste treatment and disposal, corrosion control, and environmental evaluation. For example:

- A water supply system may be large enough for a city of almost one million people. Water brought to the site is reused, often more than once, both as a conservation measure and as a way to minimize, or even eliminate, the need for wastewater discharge. Careful study of the plant mass balance makes possible the most efficient use of water and reduces the hazards of environmental impact.
- Construction materials that reduce the potential for corrosion also must be chosen by the chemical engineer. Much consideration must be given to the selection of protective coatings and the means of appropriately pretreating or chemically conditioning fluids, all with a view to reducing corrosion to acceptable limits.
- Complex process equipment is required to produce high-purity water for steam-cycle makeup. Similar equipment is required to maintain cycle fluid purity, handling flows equivalent to the water supply requirement for perhaps a quarter of a million people.

The consulting engineering field affords a wide range of opportunities for today's chemical engineering graduate. He is able to gain an understanding of civil, electrical, and mechanical engineering, and of architecture through his work with persons in these disciplines. He is given every opportunity to develop both personally and professionally, and to increase his knowledge. The chemical engineering graduate who enters the consulting engineering field provides himself with ample opportunity to become a professional engineer.

Interrelationships of Disciplines

To understand the total picture of the major disciplines in the consulting arena, it is helpful to examine the way they interrelate in the formation of a project.

For many years, the consulting engineer dealt primarily with civil works, such as roads, bridges, canals, dams, and reservoirs. There were few mechanical or electrical systems built into such projects.

As technology evolved, buildings, factories, utilities, and other facilities incorporated mechanical systems for plumbing, heating, and power, and electrical systems for lighting and energy. As each of these technologies became more sophisticated, they commanded greater attention and a greater proportion of the project, in terms of both work and costs. The newer disciplines began to take on full partnership roles. A brief review of the directories published by American Consulting Engineers Council (1979) or the National Society of Professional Engineers (1980) reveals the diversity of engineering services offered by consulting engineers in all major disciplines and specialties.

A modern office building is a good example of the growth of these new disciplines. Fifty years ago, the cost of the electrical and mechanical systems would have been a minor part of the total cost of the building. Today, however, the mechanical and electrical systems frequently account for more than half of the cost. As a result, mechanical and electrical disciplines have been incorporated into design firms serving the building construction industry.

Consulting engineering firms serving utilities and industries may combine all major disciplines and some specialties to provide complete engineering services. With the modern-day emphasis on pollution control and other environmental concerns, for example, the chemical engineer is becoming more involved in projects other than process industries.

Still, there are many firms that specialize in one discipline only. Perhaps this type of practice is most obvious in the commercial building field, sometimes referred to as "interprofessional" practice. The architect is usually the prime design professional and subcontracts structural, mechanical, and electrical systems to consulting firms specializing in those disciplines. However, there are now instances where firms are being formed to combine the mechanical and electrical disciplines, which gives the engineering firm a majority of the work and greater control of the project. On some building projects, engineering firms are replacing architects as the prime design professionals.

Consulting engineering firms exist in virtually every conceivable size and organizational structure. They are as varied as the services they provide. Some insight as to the interrelationships of the various disciplines can be gained by examining the types of practice available to the consulting engineer and by looking at some examples of how an engineer in a consulting firm might relate to engineers in other disciplines in providing professional engineering services.

The types of practice can be divided into four general categories: (1) the pure consultant, expert, or specialist—one person with a highly developed expertise; (2) a single-discipline firm in support of another discipline, or another profession, or under direct contract to the user; (3) a multidiscipline firm providing complete engineering services for complex projects involving two, three, four or more disciplines; and (4) the multiprofession firm providing not only multidiscipline engineering services but also professional services involving architecture, planning, law, science, environment, economics, and management.

Pure Consultant

The pure consultant is a professional who has developed a high degree of expertise in a particular subject. He is sought for specialized problem solving, expert testimony in courts of law, or consultation for high-level decision making. His success is determined by his level of knowledge, ability to communicate, and established credibility. Normally a one-person firm, this consultant is totally dependent on his own abilities and the demand for the expertise that he has to offer. He has a considerable amount of freedom and is not encumbered by payroll and other needs of a larger work force. On the other hand, he does not have the technical and professional support of associates or the help to carry on should he become temporarily or permanently incapacitated.

The growing complexity of technology and the concurrent growth in litigation have led to a specialty known as "forensic engineering," which is generally defined as the application of engineering science and theory to accident investigation and courtroom testimony. This type of practice requires an exceptionally high degree of knowledge in specialized areas, such as properties of materials, stress and fatigue, failures, electricity, toxic materials, soil mechanics, and all categories of electrical and mechanical systems and equipment.

Inasmuch as the pure consultant is totally dependent on his own expertise and credibility, which can be achieved only with many years of directly related experience, he is normally an alumnus of a larger design firm, an industry, or a university faculty where he had an opportunity to develop his potential. It is not the type of practice that a new graduate would expect to enter directly.

Single-Discipline Firm

The single-discipline firm concentrates the engineering talent of a single discipline and often limits its scope of service to a specialty within a discipline such as structural engineering or air-conditioning engineering. While some firms of this type contract directly with the user of the service, many provide services as subcontractors to other disciplines or to other professions, such as architects. These firms may provide a full range of services in their discipline, or they may restrict their practice to more specialized services like systems analysis or feasibility studies.

One of the most common single-discipline firms is the structural design firm that subcontracts to an architectural firm for the design of the structural systems for a building. The engineer's participation normally includes design and detailing for fabrication and construction of the building structure and, depending on the contractual relationship with the architect, may also include participation in the conceptual design, cost estimating, and observation of construction. The structural engineer must work closely with other engineering subcontractors: with the soil specialist or geotechnical engineer regarding foundations, and with the mechanical and electrical engineers to coordinate floor loadings and accommodate space requirements. Although the architect has final responsibility for overall coordination, the engineer must use his own initiative and develop a close communication with the other subcontractors to avoid interferences and other discrepancies.

Some of the other disciplines or specialties frequently practiced in single-discipline firms include soil mechanics and geotechnical, traffic, acoustical, electrical, mechanical, mining, and transportation engineering.

Multidiscipline Firm

Multidiscipline firms have developed in response to projects requiring integrated engineering disciplines. Power plants are a good example of projects involving virtually all phases of civil, mechanical, and electrical, as well as chemical, engineering in the highly sophisticated water treatment and pollution control processes. The intimate and complex relationships of the disciplines require a degree of coordination and communication that can be accomplished effectively only under singular management. While in most firms the individual disciplines are segregated in sections or departments to develop and maintain a high level of technical capability, they are integrated as one team within the project organization, interfacing closely and coordinating their individual efforts to produce a unified result.

The sample project organization chart (Figure 2–1) for a multidiscipline project might apply to the design of a power plant, a refinery, or another large industrial complex. This organization constitutes a "team" or "task force" dedicated specifically to the project at hand. Each discipline has its defined responsibilities plus the responsibility

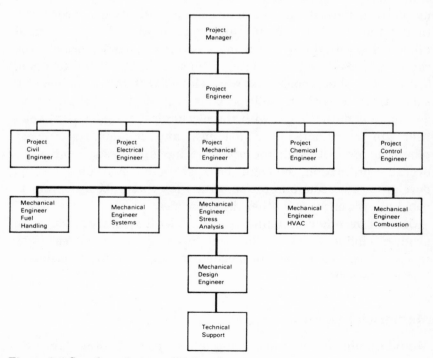

Figure 2–1 Sample project organization chart.

of coordinating its design with that of each of the other disciplines. While the overall coordination of the project is the responsibility of the project engineer, it is not possible for all coordination and decisions to be handled by one person. Consequently, most of the coordination is accomplished by the design engineers communicating across discipline lines, and only the major coordinating decisions are referred to the project engineer. Such projects require a high degree of teamwork and initiative on the part of each individual with design responsibility. The individual must have a thorough understanding of his own discipline and at least a working knowledge of each of the other disciplines with which he must interface.

A project team or task force is dispersed upon completion of its mission, and the various members are reassigned to another project team or task force, often in different capacities but still with the primary goal of using their knowledge and skills in concert with other engineers to produce a successful, coordinated engineering effort.

Multiprofession Firm

Multiprofession firms are a relatively recent development. They go one step further than the multidiscipline firms and include not only the various disciplines of engineering but also the disciplines of other professions such as architecture, planning, law, science, or management. The advent of environmental and economic impact studies, federal regulations, grant programs, the space program, and the energy program has engendered a coalition of many professions to address the broad spectrum of concerns. Modern siting of an industrial facility draws upon the expertise of biologists, meteorologists, zoologists, archaeologists, geologists, sociologists, economists, planners, engineers, lawyers, and public relations personnel. Certainly it is not necessary for each firm to employ all of these different experts. Indeed, many experts are retained as individual consultants in the capacity defined as pure consultant. However, the trend has been for large firms to place these multiprofession experts on their payrolls to maintain control, to be sure that the capability is readily available when needed, and to demonstrate the firm's ability to handle specific projects.

The project organization in a multiprofession firm is very similar to that of the multidiscipline firm. The firm's representatives of other professions may contribute as a team or as individuals depending on the degree of services provided. For example, architects normally contribute as a design team, whereas the meteorologist or economist is more often an individual contributor. In either case, the contributions of all professions must be blended skillfully to assure a smooth, successful project.

Diversity and Challenge

No matter what discipline he has selected, the graduating engineer will find that consulting engineering offers diversity and challenges. There is a place for the engineer with a high degree of expertise who wants to practice forensic engineering or consult in a highly specialized area. There also is a place for the engineer who wants to be a part of a team highly skilled and competent in the practice of a common discipline or a team involving several disciplines and perhaps other technologies and professions as well.

Consulting engineering offers opportunities to design new systems and facilities, to analyze existing engineering works and evaluate economic feasibilities, and to administer contracts or manage construction. It is an excellent career choice for the engineer who likes working with people to develop concepts, solve problems, improve the environment, enhance the quality of life, conserve and make the most effective use of our resources, and bring together all of the skills and solutions that technology can provide. There are diversity and depth in consulting engineering—long- and short-term assignments, projects of varying size and scope, individual and team effort, and relationships with both staff and clients.

Graduating engineers, whether they choose civil, mechanical, electrical, or chemical engineering, will do well to investigate closely the opportunities in consulting engineering. Working as a team, engineers of all disciplines have the opportunity to accomplish major engineering works which will affect a single business or an entire industry, a community or an entire region, or perhaps an entire nation. There is opportunity to be a manager with all of the challenges of planning, organization, staffing, allocation of time and resources, cost control, quality assurance, and profitability, but with the primary purpose of providing professional engineering services to meet client and public needs.

Consulting engineering provides engineers in all major disciplines with a rare opportunity to practice engineering as a true profession, to be a manager, and to aspire to become, and eventually to become, an entrepreneur.

References

American Consulting Engineers Council. *1979 Directory.* Washington, D.C.: Author, 1978.

"Civil Engineering Needs Definition," *Engineering News-Record,* June 6, 1963, p. 26.

Cross, Hardy. In Robert C. Goodpasture (Ed.), *Engineers and Ivory Towers* (1st ed.). New York: McGraw-Hill Book Co., 1952.

de Camp, L. Sprague. *The Ancient Engineers.* New York: Ballantine Books, Inc., 1974.

Florman, Samuel C. *The Existential Pleasures of Engineering.* New York: St. Martin's Press, 1976.

Frontinus, Sextus Julius. *The Water Supply of the City of Rome* (Clemens Herschel, trans.). Boston: New England Water Works Association, 1973.

Hoy, Suellen M. "The Profession in Perspective," chap. 20, *History of Public Works in the United States.* Chicago: American Public Works Association, 1976.

National Society of Professional Engineers. *1980–81 Directory of Engineers in Private Practice.* Washington, D.C.: Professional Engineers in Private Practice (a division of the National Society of Professional Engineers), 1980.

Thorndike, Joseph J. (Ed.). *Discovery of Lost Worlds.* New York: American Heritage Publishing Co., 1979.

"What's Going on in CE Education," *Engineering New-Record,* June 6, 1963, pp. 25–30.

Wisely, William H. *The American Civil Engineer.* New York: American Society of Civil Engineers, 1974.

Chapter

3

THE CONSULTING ENGINEER'S CLIENTS

C. Richard Walter
President, Hazen and Sawyer, P.C.

Who Is A Client?

A client is a person or organization that hires a consulting engineer to solve an engineering problem or to perform an engineering service. Sometimes a client does not know whether he has an engineering problem or not, and he consults with an engineer to make a determination. For example, a metal plating or paint manufacturing firm may become aware that the government has passed regulations governing the handling and disposal of hazardous wastes. The company will engage a consulting engineer knowledgeable about process wastes and the regulations governing their disposal to study the situation and determine whether the firm is affected by the new regulations. The consulting engineer will review the company's chemical analyses of its waste, or perhaps take additional samples and make other analyses, to see if the waste is classified as hazardous. At this point, the consulting engineer may find that the company's wastes are not considered hazardous within the definition of the regulations and that there is little likelihood that hazardous wastes would be produced in the future unless major product or production changes were made. A report to the client of this finding would complete the assignment. If the consulting engineer finds that the company's wastes are hazardous, the client will probably authorize him to develop a program to reduce or eliminate the waste, either to render it nonhazardous or to dispose of it in an acceptable manner. On such an assignment the engineer truly acts as a consultant to the client, advising him on technical matters without actually designing physical facilities.

On other occasions, the client knows what he wants to accomplish and engages a consulting engineer to advise him how to do so and to design the facilities required. A developing country may know that it can grow a particular crop in a fertile inland region and market it internationally at a good profit if it could develop a way to transport the crop to a seaport city efficiently and economically. That nation would probably retain a consulting engineer to study the problem and evaluate alternative means of transportation. The consulting engineer would make feasibility analyses and cost comparisons of transport by road, by railroad, and perhaps by conveyor system or by airplane, depending upon the type of crop and the distance over which it must be transported. In making the analysis, he might call upon experts in such fields as agricultural production and marketing to develop projections of traffic volume, or geologists and soils experts to assist in the determination of the feasibility and cost of constructing the alternative transportation systems. The consulting engineer would then prepare a report detailing his analyses and findings and recommending to the client the most cost-effective transportation arrangement. After the client reviewed the report and made a selection he would probably authorize the engineer to perform the design work.

Some clients know exactly what they need and engage a consulting engineer to design and oversee the construction of a specific facility. For instance, a manufacturer may need to expand his plant. He knows the overall size, the necessary inside ceiling height or overhead clearance, the desirable column spacing, and the inside environmental conditions to be maintained. The consulting engineer is engaged to define the structural system for the building, the type and size of foundation, the architectural treatment, the roofing system, the electrical system, and the heating and ventilating systems. All these must be reduced to a set of plans and specifications from which contractors can bid and construct the facility. For such an assignment, some large consulting firms might provide all the requisite services in-house while others may draw upon other engineers to provide specialized service under a subcontract arrangement.

Client Profile

Consulting engineers work for a great variety of clients, including private industry, public bodies such as commissions or authorities, the federal government, state and local governments, foreign governments, other engineers or architects, and occasionally private individuals.

The type of practice a consulting engineer engages in determines to a large extent the type of client he will serve. A civil engineer, specializing in the design of bridges, is likely to have a clientele consisting chiefly of state and local governments or perhaps autono-

TABLE 3-1

Consulting Engineering Firms and Their Clients

CLIENT	SMALL FIRMS (1–25 EMPLOYEES)		MEDIUM FIRMS (26–100 EMPLOYEES)		LARGE FIRMS (101-PLUS EMPLOYEES)		TOTAL FIRMS	
	NO.	%	NO.	%	NO.	%	NO.	%
Private business	7,948	94.1	1,713	94.5	551	87.7	10,213	93.8
Utility	2,811	33.3	1,019	56.2	408	65.0	4,238	38.9
Institutions	3,599	42.6	964	53.2	334	53.2	4,897	44.9
Federal government	2,805	33.2	1,111	61.3	420	66.9	4,336	39.8
State government	3,151	37.3	1,148	63.3	376	59.9	4,675	42.9
Local government	5,034	59.6	1,388	76.6	402	64.0	6,824	62.6
Subtotal, government*	5,721	67.7	1,501	82.6	489	77.9	7,711	70.8
Architects	5,181	61.3	1,014	55.9	236	37.6	6,431	59.0
Other consulting firms	4,480	57.3	1,045	57.6	302	48.1	6,187	56.8
Contractors	4,216	49.9	926	51.1	284	45.2	5,426	49.8
Subtotal, firms†	8,450	. . .	1,813	. . .	628	. . .	10,891	

SOURCE: Compiled from *Consulting Engineer* June 1980.

*This subtotal represents the number of consulting firms engaged in any level of government consulting. There is an overlap because some firms engage in consulting at more than one government level.

†This subtotal represents the number of consulting firms retained by other firms. There is an overlap because some firms work with more than one category of client firms.

mous highway or bridge authorities. On the other hand, mechanical engineers specializing in the heating and air conditioning of buildings may serve many different types of clients. They may serve as subcontract consultants to architects designing new buildings, or they may directly serve industry, school boards, or various levels of government in making studies and redesigns for existing structures, and, on occasion, they may even do work on stores or residences owned by private individuals.

The most recent survey by *Consulting Engineer* magazine of a total of 10,891 consulting engineering firms listed the number of these firms serving various categories of clients (Table 3–1). It can be seen that most consulting firms, regardless of size, include private businesses (companies and individuals) among their clientele. Also, the larger firms are more likely to serve governmental clients or utilities, while small firms more often perform interprofessional work for architects.

Reasons for Engaging Consulting Engineers

Consulting engineers are engaged by clients for many reasons or combinations of reasons. These can include:

1. *No engineering capability of their own.* Builders, private individuals, manufacturing organizations, and even some levels of government may have no engineering capability of their own and utilize consulting engineers for all their engineering work. These clients rarely have occasion to use engineers, and keeping engineers on staff would make little sense when they can be engaged on a job-by-job basis as needed.

Thus, the owner of a building who discovers cracks in the walls will seek the services of a consultant to diagnose the cause and develop a corrective program. A school board seeking an energy study and development of an energy conservation program normally will engage a consulting engineer to undertake the work. In these instances, the client could hire engineers as part of his staff to do the necessary work, but the time delay, the uncertainty of finding competent engineers on an ad hoc basis, and the necessity to release them after the assignment is completed all make this course of action unattractive. On the other hand, he can engage a consulting engineer who has demonstrated expertise and experience in the type of assignment and who has staff and facilities available to undertake it. Upon completion of the work, the owner is not further obligated to the consultant and has not incurred continuing overhead expense.

2. *Engineering staff not qualified in work area.* Frequently, a client will have an in-house engineering department, but the staff is not skilled in the discipline required for a particular assignment. A plant engineering department of a manufacturer may be competent to design or modify manufacturing and materials-handling equipment for a plant expansion, but he will need to hire a consulting engineer to design a building addition, including climate control facilities, to house the equipment. The manufacturer has a continuing need for his plant engineering department but only sporadic needs for building design skill. He finds it is not economical to retain such skill in-house, and so he obtains it from the outside professional, the consulting engineer. Similarly, many municipal public works or engineering departments are staffed to design the routine water and sewer line additions to the municipal system. They develop an expertise in this work because of its recurring nature and through an intimate knowledge of their community, the streets along which the proposed lines must run, and the other facilities and subsurface conditions to be encountered. On the other hand, the municipality will need to build a water or wastewater treatment plant only once every 10 or 20 years, and then it wants one that incorporates the latest technology. It is not efficient, or perhaps not even possible, for the municipal engineering staff to keep abreast of the latest design practices in such a specialized field or to design such complex facilities in an efficient, cost-effective manner. Here again, the client may know exactly the type of facility he wishes but finds it more efficient to have it designed by a consulting engineer.

3. *In-house engineering staff sized for normal work load.* Some clients have a fully qualified in-house engineering staff that would be capable of undertaking a new special assignment, but they cannot spare the time from their regular workload. Many clients who find themselves in this position give the new assignment to a consulting engineering firm rather than attempt to build up their in-house staff to handle the peak workload. They find this more economical and efficient than hiring new personnel, training them for the task at hand, providing supervisory personnel from the busy permanent staff, and then releasing the new people when the special assignment has been completed. For example, a state highway department might need to undertake an extensive bridge repair program to be completed over a two- or three-year period. The department may have been doing such work at a more limited pace, but decides that engaging consulting engineers is the most efficient and cost-effective way to handle the temporary peak workload.

4. *Desire for outside expert opinion.* Often a client engages a consulting engineer in order to obtain the opinion of an acknowledged expert not directly associated with the client or the project. The most obvious example would be the use of a consulting engineer to act as an expert witness in a product liability suit or an accident case. The testimony of an employee-engineer would not be nearly as effective, since it would be subject to question as to objectivity and freedom from prejudice. In another instance, an industry or municipality seeking to issue bonds for financing a specific project might retain a consulting engineer to prepare a feasibility report and engineering evaluation of the project. The report would be used by prospective bond underwriters and investors to assist them in determining the worth of the project and the bonds. For assignments such as these, the prior experiences and reputation of the engineer engaged are of great importance in determining the value or weight of his expert opinion.

5. *Economy.* One of the most common reasons for clients engaging the services of consulting engineers is the recognition that it is usually the least expensive way to accomplish an engineering task. The consulting engineering firm is able to quickly put to work a team of engineers and support staff trained and experienced in the assignment at hand. Such a team can undertake and complete the project much more efficiently than an in-house staff. The in-house staff normally works on other matters and would need to spend considerable time and money researching the problem and its possible solutions. The consulting engineer, handling similar assignments regularly, can productively start on the project immediately upon being engaged. If a true cost analysis is made, taking into account all the overhead costs of the in-house staff—such as fringe benefits, costs of office space, management overhead costs, and nonproductive time— it usually will be found that the engagement of a consulting engineering firm is the most economical way to accomplish an engineering task.

Interprofessional Work

In addition to the usual direct engagement of consulting engineers, there is also a considerable amount of interprofessional work in which consulting engineers are engaged by other engineers or fellow professionals to assist them on an assignment. In these instances, one professional serves as the "prime," and the other provides services under a subcontract arrangement to help accomplish the assignment. Perhaps the most common example of this is an architect commissioned to design a building who engages a team of other professionals, principally engineers, to assist him on the assignment. These usually will include a structural engineer, who will be responsible for the design of the building's foundation and structural framework; an electrical engineer, who will design the building's electrical power and lighting systems; and a mechanical engineer who specializes in the design of heating, ventilating, and air-conditioning systems.

Depending upon the nature of the project and its complexity, other design professionals may be added to the team. If a proposed structure is especially large or the foundation conditions at the site are unusual or difficult, a soils and foundation consultant would probably be engaged. For concert halls or other theaters for the performing arts, an acoustical consultant might be called in. For the design of a university campus building or the design of municipal or industrial buildings on large sites, the services of a landscape architect might be required. The combined effort of such a group of design professionals, when one engages the others to give the client the best possible design for his money, is known as interprofessional practice.

On most nonindustrial and even some industrial jobs the architect is hired by the owner as the prime professional, and he in turn engages the others under a subcontract arrangement. Sometimes there is a third tier, as when a foundation consultant is retained as a subcontractor by the structural engineer, who himself is a subcontractor to the architect. The prime professional has the direct contract with the owner and the responsibility to put together a team with the requisite skills to accomplish the assignment. It is his job to coordinate the work of the other team members and make certain that it is done in a timely and satisfactory manner and that the requirements of the client are satisfied.

Most clients are not knowledgeable enough about the various tasks to be performed and their interrelationships to separately contract and coordinate a team of professionals. The client looks to the architect, or other prime professional, to provide the basic design to suit his needs and to select other competent professionals to assist him in meeting the client's goals. To attain these goals, the architect needs the expertise and experience of the consulting engineers and other team members. Consulting engineers are well-versed in their roles on such an assignment, and a competent prime professional can coordinate their efforts into one efficient design team.

Overseas Work

Engineers are being called upon increasingly to provide engineering services in foreign countries. A U.S. engineer may be asked by a drug company which is one of his regular clients to do engineering work on a pharmaceutical plant located in a foreign country. The engineer had worked on two other pharmaceutical plants for the same client in the United States and is familiar with the processes and packaging operations involved, as well as the types of equipment and material standards the company uses. The management and in-house engineering staff of the company know the capability of the consultant and feel confident he will do a good job. The consultant might choose to engage the assistance of an engineer in the foreign country to advise him on local practices and codes or the availability of certain types of material and labor. The client is thereby assured of competent engineering adapted to the foreign environment.

Similarly, the U.S. government or armed services will usually engage a U.S. engineering firm to work on an overseas base or other facility. In many instances, governmental regulations or the facility authorization will require that all services be provided by U.S. firms.

Even without such a requirement, a U.S. firm would most likely be hired to assure compatibility with other U.S. facilities and equipment. Again, the owner seeks to continue a relationship with the consulting engineer, or the type of consulting engineer, he is accustomed to working with on domestic assignments.

Frequently, foreign countries or other clients have specialized engineering assignments to be performed for which there are no local engineering resources. This is particularly prevalent in developing countries which often must seek foreign help for such projects as port facilities, bridges, sophisticated government buildings, or hotels. Most such countries want, and will insist upon receiving, facilities of first-rate modern design. American engineering expertise continues to play a leading role in such foreign development work.

Foreign work requires, in addition to the basic engineering expertise, a knowledge of and appreciation for the special needs and conditions in the foreign country. In many instances, plans and specifications must be prepared in a foreign language and with a knowledge of the technical limitations of foreign contractors and facility-operating personnel. Such assignments are especially challenging and professionally rewarding.

Relationship with the Client

The consulting engineer's relationship with the client should be one of trust; he should be viewed as an advisor in whom the client has confidence. This type of relationship takes time to develop. A client may select a consulting engineer on the basis of his specialized training and previous experience which seems to qualify him for the assignment at hand, but the client usually will have some initial qualms or anxiety. This often will be true even if the consultant is highly recommended by associates of the client who have used his services. It is only after the client has met with the consulting engineer several times and has learned firsthand how the consultant views matters, how he approaches a problem, and how he candidly and capably reports his findings, that the client will feel truly confident.

It is this feeling of trust and confidence that causes clients to return to consultants they had previously utilized when they are again in need of engineering services. Such repeat engagements for clients frequently make up a large portion of a consulting engineer's practice, and most consulting engineers try to keep in touch with clients and review how well their designs have met the clients' needs.

Many clients will return to a consulting engineer with whom they have developed a relationship of trust and confidence for problems or assignments that they know are outside his usual area of practice. In such cases, they expect him to put together a team with the requisite skills to undertake the assignment, or to refer the client to another engineer who the consultant knows will be suited for the job. Referrals of this nature are another principal source of assignments for many consulting engineers.

Responsibility to the Client

The consulting engineer's responsibility to his client can be summed up by saying it is to act as a faithful agent of the client on engineering matters. A consulting engineer's highest obligation is to protect the safety, health, and welfare of the public in the performance of his professional duties. Within that overall framework, consulting engineers must operate their practices so as to serve the best interests of their clients. American Consulting Engineers Council has Rules of Practice which all its members are expected to follow. Those governing consulting engineers' responsibilities to their clients include:

- Consulting engineers shall undertake assignments only when qualified by education or experience in the specific technical fields involved.
- Consulting engineers may accept an assignment outside of their fields of competence to the extent that their services are restricted to those phases of the project in which they are qualified and to the extent that they are satisfied that all other phases of such project will be performed by registered or otherwise qualified associates, consultants, or employees, in which case they may then sign the documents for the total project.
- Consulting engineers shall disclose all known or potential conflicts of interests to their clients by promptly informing them of any business

association, interest or other circumstances which could influence or appear to influence their judgment or the quality of their services.

- Consulting engineers shall not accept compensation, financial or otherwise, from more than one party for services on the same project, or for services pertaining to the same project, unless the circumstances are fully disclosed to, and agreed to, by all interested parties.
- Consulting engineers shall not reveal facts, data, or information obtained in a professional capacity without the prior consent of the client except as authorized or required by law or these Guidelines.

Professional Liability

As with other professionals, a consulting engineer is professionally and legally obligated to provide services reflecting competence in the engineering principles involved and diligence and care in their application. Engineering, although not an exact science, is chiefly based on scientific principles and principles of safe practice developed over the years. All engineers are expected to know and abide by such principles. Courts have ruled that consulting engineers have a professional liability for errors or omissions which harm the client or the public. Careful supervision of the work of subordinates and checking of the final work product is expected of all consulting engineers. Perfection cannot be guaranteed, but all reasonable care must be taken to protect the public and the client.

Since consulting engineers are responsible for damages caused by professional errors or omissions they may commit, their potential financial liability can be great. Often this potential liability exceeds the engineer's total fee on an assignment, or even the construction cost of the project. To protect the public and the financial survival of their practice, most consulting engineers carry professional liability insurance coverage. Usually, this is arranged so that the consulting engineer personally must pay any losses or damages up to a certain amount, with the liability insurance carrier available to cover possible large awards. Attention to quality control and provision of adequate insurance to protect the public are important aspects of the consulting engineer's practice. Without them, no consulting engineer could stay in business very long.

Serving the Private Client

Many different types of clients are included in the classification "private client." This sector of the consultant's market includes manufacturers of all types; process industries; transportation companies such as airlines and railroads; commercial concerns such as banks, insurance companies, and department stores; property developers and builders; individual property or building owners; and almost any other kind of private organization or enterprise.

To be engaged for a proposed project by a prospective client who is the owner or manager of some private enterprise, the consulting engineer must demonstrate that he can do the job better and at lower cost than the client's own central engineering staff. If the client's firm is a large one, and he has in his employ a great many engineers of recognized ability, he may be startled at the idea that the consultant considers himself superior to the company's staff engineers. On the other hand, the owner of a medium-sized plant with a relatively small engineering staff may acknowledge the special talents of the consultant and realize that he does not have these talents available within his own organization. But he frequently feels that his own engineers can do a satisfactory job, and he is sure the cost would be much less.

Owners of small industrial plants readily acknowledge the need for outside engineering services, but all too frequently they are of the opinion that these services can be provided by contractors or by way of "free engineering" from manufacturers.

The engineer must demonstrate to these clients, regardless of the sizes of their organizations, that outside, independent engineering services result in better projects at lower cost. Design and supervision of new construction is a special type of engineering work. It is only logical that a good firm of engineers, doing 3 to 30 major construction jobs every year, can do better work at lower cost than equally competent engineers on the company staff who are called upon to design one new project every 30 years. A consulting engineering firm works on design, specification, and supervision of construction day after day, month after month. The central engineering headquarters' staff is engaged primarily in operation and maintenance work. The consulting engineer, therefore, offers his private client broader and more thorough experience in new project work than the client could possibly get from his own engineering employees. Even very large industrial firms with large engineering departments find it more efficient to utilize the services of consulting engineers for the design and construction supervision of new plants, offices, and other facilities.

It is not a matter of the consulting engineer and his staff being better engineers than the client's in-house engineering department, but that the consulting engineer is more qualified in his own particular field while the employee engineers probably are more qualified in theirs. The preparation of specifications and contract documents is everyday work for the consultant, yet it is an unusual undertaking for the average in-house engineering staff. Company engineers seldom are accustomed to dealing with contractors or with construction blueprints. Also, the consulting engineer can apply concentration to his projects that cannot be matched by engineers in the company's own plant. The consulting engineer does not have the distractions of day-by-day routine or the incidental problems that plague plant engineers.

Having been engaged by a private client to design a project such as a plant expansion, the consulting engineer must develop a good relationship with the client's in-house engineering staff. The in-house staff knows the particular problems and needs of the client's operations, which the consulting engineer must learn in order to design an efficient plant. On the other hand, the consultant brings to the assignment a fresh outlook and knowledge learned from prior projects. No matter how intelligent and well-trained an employee engineer may be, if he has been working in one plant and under one management for years, he will find it difficult to look at a project objectively. The consultant is not so handicapped. For him the project is not in any way tied to past production or maintenance practices. While this lack of familiarity with past procedure may have its difficulties, some of the consultant's new ideas are frequently of practical value. He might bring ideas gained from the design of an automobile parts manufacturing plant to the layout and design of a warehouse materials handling system for a food distributor. The engineering staff of the food distributor probably never had the opportunity to examine closely the design of an automobile parts plant and to learn things applicable to their own operations.

An in-house engineering staff will learn that the consulting engineer can be of great assistance to them in a number of ways. One way is to help the staff gain management acceptance of new ideas that up until that time had been turned down. The consulting engineer, as an outside expert, often carries great weight with management, and the staff engineer will appreciate having the weight of independent expert advice on his side. Therefore, the staff engineer and the consultant can be mutually helpful to each other and, in the process, helpful to the client. The wise consultant knows that good relations with the staff engineers are extremely important to the success of his project.

Serving the Public Sector

Serving clients in the public sector is quite different from serving clients in the private sector or doing interprofessional work. In the latter cases, the relationship usually is much more flexible and governed by what appears to be the most efficient way of proceeding. Work for the public sector, on the other hand, is paid for with public funds and is under the responsibility of public officials. It generally is more constrained by regulations or time-honored procedures developed to protect the public and the officeholders.

The private client is in business to make a profit and is receptive to approaches and suggestions from consulting engineers who can help him maximize his profits. The private client can retain the consulting engineer of his choice, so long as he can satisfy his higher management that a good job will be done at a fair price.

Clients in the public sector have no profit motive. At the elective office level they are motivated by a desire to please their electorate as much as the desire to do what they think will benefit the public. There is a strong motive to avoid any actions for which they might be criticized. Invariably, there is a preference to "play it safe" rather than to take chances. Things are done the way they were done in the past, and there is little incentive to try something new if any risk is involved.

The first point at which this difference is detected is the selection and engagement of engineers. In the private sector or in interprofessional practice, consulting engineers present their qualifications to potential clients in an informal manner and the clients are free to choose whichever engineer they wish. Some of the larger industries keep consulting engineers' qualification packages in their files, indexed by areas of specialization. When a consulting engineer is needed, a small number of firms are invited to present specific qualifications for the particular assignment. The private client is free to repeatedly use the same consulting firm if he is satisfied with its work.

Consultant selection is quite a bit different in the public sector. On the local level—for small municipalities and towns—selection usually is limited to local firms well known by the elected officials. Geographic location and involvement in community affairs often are more important than superior qualifications. The assignments are usually not too complex, and special expertise or staffing is not a strong factor in the selection.

At the higher levels of the public sector—larger cities, counties, and state and federal agencies—selection of consulting engineers tends to be much more formalized. Engineers are requested, by printed public announcement, to submit specific qualifications for a particular job. Specific selection criteria, which evaluate the firms competitively, are established and they are often stated in the announcement. The criteria may include, in addition to expertise and experience in the field involved, such things as firm location, previous assignments for the agency, extent of minority employment, and present office workload. The firms are then rated against the criteria by a consultant-rating committee and a short list of the three to seven top-ranked firms is developed. Often these finalists are invited to an interview where they make a presentation and answer questions, or they are asked to submit a detailed proposal of how they would do the work if selected. In some instances, they are asked to estimate the work effort or cost involved, although that is generally acknowledged to be a poor criterion for selection for professional services. The selection procedure is detailed and complicated, designed to assure the public that it is an objective procedure free of favoritism.

Once the consulting engineer is selected, the terms of the contract, at least for the larger public entities, are complex. The terms are usually quite one-sided, with the public body maintaining the more favorable position. The contract, or at least the general conditions portion, is prepared by the public agency's legal staff and is designed to give maximum protection to the agency and the public. The consulting engineer must depend upon the reasonable interpretation of the contract by the client during the course of the work.

Fees obtained for work in the public sector generally are somewhat lower than those obtained for work in the private sector and frequently are more closely tied to a specific scope of work. Any adjustments in work to be performed because of unforeseen circumstances will most likely require a formal scope change and fee modification. On the other hand, contracts usually cannot be entered into by the public bodies unless the necessary funds have been specifically appropriated, and fee payments tend to be more secure and more regular than in the private sector.

Working relationships with the public-sector client and his staff vary greatly. On the smaller, more local level, the client may have a minimal or no engineering staff, and the consultant is directly responsible to the local administration or elected officials. Often, the engineer must attend all local governing body meetings to answer any questions which may arise concerning the project. The public officials specifically look to the consultant to ensure that the public is satisfied not only with the end product but also with the work as it progresses, and that the public is not unduly inconvenienced.

Larger public agencies have engineering staffs of their own and the consultant usually reports to them. This provides better guidance to the consultant on local preferences and procedures, and the consultant interfaces with engineers who can understand technical matters better than most elected officials. Sometimes the public agency engineering staff resents the work's being given out to the consultant instead of being done in-house. Public department heads often believe that their salaries will increase with the size of their staffs. Many are more interested in building the size of their departments than in finding the most economical or efficient approach to each project. This attitude can be a major problem to consulting engineers working for the public sector, and they must become adept at overcoming it. The department head and his superiors must be persuaded that their position and salary should be dependent upon the work volume handled by the department. It is far better to have a smaller number of higher-salaried staff engineers coordinating the work of outside consultants than to have a large staff of lower-level engineers and technicians doing the work in-house.

Public agency staffs are not apt to accept the presence of a consulting engineer too quickly. Often, the staff feels that the consultant is doing work they should be doing and is a threat to their jobs or their advancement to greater responsibility. Perhaps, in even more cases, there is a fear that the work of the outside expert will reflect poorly on the standards or work performed by the in-house staff. The agency staff may have been doing something the same way successfully for many years when the consultant arrives with a new method or design that he has developed or learned on another assignment. The new method may save much staff engineering time, or the new design may provide a better solution to an engineering problem at lower cost. It is only human nature to resent being outperformed. It is therefore necessary that the consultant should work with the agency staff, learn their methods, involve them in the development of the new approaches and designs, and otherwise gain their confidence. Patience, openness, and a showing of respect for the agency staff will overcome the difficulty and produce a mutually satisfying working relationship between the two groups of professionals. Once this has been attained, the interplay of ideas and experiences becomes an asset to the client.

Serving the Interprofessional Client

The prime professional makes initial contact with the client to learn his needs, develop the scope of the work, and determine the overall fee for the assignment. These are important responsibilities and can mean the difference between a successful project and one that is disappointing to the client or to the engineering team. Except for the most routine type of assignment, it is essential that the prime professional bring his consulting engineer team members into the project at the earliest possible time so that they may contribute to the development of the scope of the work.

Most clients do not initially know the various options or alternatives that should be studied and compared before a basic design arrangement is settled upon. Various combinations of basic layout and architectural design, structural framing arrangement, and mechanical systems must be evaluated before the scope can be truly fixed and the overall fee determined. All the professionals on the design team should be involved during this critical phase.

In projects involving interprofessional relationships the setting of the overall fee for assignments is an important step that greatly affects all the team members. Once the fee is set, each participating member's fee is a portion of the whole. None can gain an increase in fee without a compensating decrease in the fees of the other participants. During the past decade or so the engineering requirements of projects have become more complex, and a greater proportion of the overall fee than was previously customary has had to be allocated to the consulting engineer team members. Such rearrangement of the traditional fee division has required mutual understanding and trust among the prime professional and the other team members.

On industrial projects, where the design of the process and needed equipment is the prime objective, the building layout and structural arrangement are dictated chiefly by the process requirements, and architectural design must be accomplished within those constraints. On such assignments the architect is usually a subcontractor to a prime consulting engineer.

On other projects, where two or more disciplines are of about equal importance, it has become increasingly common for consulting engineers and architects to form joint ventures to undertake the work. Under a joint venture arrangement, the principal professionals are together directly responsible to the client for the entire project. Thus, the construction of an airport or military base, encompassing heavy site development, road and runway design, utility design, and the design of numerous buildings is often undertaken by a joint venture of a civil engineering consulting firm and an architectural firm. The client then deals directly with both the engineer and the architect. The engineer and the architect are equals, and the client is better assured of a fully coordinated design, without one discipline taking precedence at the expense of the other.

Another arrangement which has evolved to accommodate this type of assignment is the architect-engineer (A-E) or engineer-architect (E-A) firm. This type of firm is often created by the merger of two firms of different disciplines which found themselves compatible and complementary while working together in joint venture. In these firms, neither architect nor engineer is dominant, but each has equal management responsibility.

Regardless of the arrangement, it is clear that there will be a continuing need for consulting engineers and architects to work closely together to serve their clients. The complexity of projects and the regulations governing their accomplishment will require close interprofessional cooperation. An understanding of each other's roles and capabilities, coupled with the willingess to subordinate individual roles to the team effort on the client's behalf, is vital in interprofessional work.

Chapter

THE CONSULTING ENGINEER'S OFFICE

William W. Moore,
Founding Partner, Dames & Moore

To provide consulting engineering services, it is necessary to have an office where the work is done and where clients can be received. Individual engineers may use a portion of their residences or lease space in a building in the community. As consulting engineering firms grow and expand their services, they need more office space to accommodate employees and principals. But whether it is one room or a suite of offices, the consulting engineer's office is the engineer's "face" to the outside world. The appearance of the office reflects the character of the firm to visitors, to prospective clients, and even to the staff. An office that creates an impression of an efficient, businesslike operation gives a feeling of confidence and solidarity.

In leasing office space and hiring people, consulting engineers find they are operating a business. There are bills to pay, payrolls to meet, and accounting records to be maintained. Legal matters, such as leases, contracts with clients for services, and contracts with suppliers for their goods and services, must be reviewed. If the business is to be successful, it must be organized and managed properly. The consulting engineer must either learn how to manage a business or delegate its management to others.

Organizing and managing a service business is different from managing a business that produces a product. The principal element of production in a consulting engineering business is people, whereas raw materials and machines are the major elements of production in a manufacturing business.

Until recently there were only a few formal educational programs developed specifically for engineering managers. Engineers seeking training in management usually attended business schools whose programs were oriented toward the large manufacturing or banking institutions rather than toward the specific problems of organizing and managing a consulting engineering business. The same was true of most seminar programs offered by management organizations.

In the last 5 to 10 years, however, the situation has changed and there are greater educational opportunities for engineers to obtain management training related to their specific needs. Several engineering schools have developed courses for management training of engineers, at both the undergraduate and graduate levels. Organizations such as American Consulting Engineers Council (ACEC) provide seminars and home-study courses to help the engineer learn the arts and skills of managing a consulting engineering business.

Most consulting engineering businesses start as small organizations with one or two engineers and a secretary. At this stage, there is little need for organization and management. The engineers contact potential clients, obtain contracts, and perform the engineering work required. The secretary establishes filing systems, does the bookkeeping, acts as a receptionist, and types letters and reports. The record keeping is simple and there usually are few communications problems, since each member of the group knows what the others are doing most of the time; information retrieval often is based on the memories of the people.

As the business grows and the firm becomes involved in larger and more complex projects, the simple office systems of the small organization are no longer adequate. If the consulting engineering business is to be successful as it grows, attention must be given to organization, management, and profit. Some engineers may feel that organizing and managing a business for profit is a distasteful concept. Their interests are in engineering and their motivation is to do the best engineering jobs possible for their clients. Such motivation is a very strong and important part of the engineering profession. However, if the business part of providing services is not given attention and the business fails through lack of profitability, the engineers lose their opportunities to perform the engineering services from which they derive their satisfaction. Thus, profit is an important element in a consulting engineering business.

Organization

The oldest form of organization developed by people is the "pyramid" type, which probably started with the formation of tribes within primitive societies. The most successful hunters and/or the strongest fighters became the chiefs of the tribes. The chiefs designated others to oversee the activities of the tribes, and these people became middle managers. In many tribal societies there was a council of elders who advised the chief and helped make decisions for the tribes' activities, somewhat similar to boards of directors in today's corporations.

The tribal pyramid concept was adopted by the Roman legions in the organization of their armies and their government. They organized on the basis of units of 10. One squad leader would have 10 people under his command; a centurion would have 10 squad leaders and 100 men under his command. Units of 10 probably are the basis of the term "span of control" used in modern organizational theory, the theory being that 10 people are the most that one person can effectively supervise without other levels of management. The pyramid concept of organization builds upward to an apex of one person who may be the commanding general in a military organization or the chief executive officer in an industrial organization.

The ideas about organization have not changed greatly since the times of the tribal chiefs and the Roman legions. We see today many industrial, military, and governmental organizations which are pyramidal in form. Most organizational charts, which are graphic illustrations of the lines of command, or lines of authority, are pyramids, having a broad base and an apex. When organizations have simple missions to perform and all members understand their roles in accomplishing the missions and willingly carry out the orders that they receive from their superiors in the pyramid, the pyramid organization works efficiently. However, in more complex situations, things can become muddled. Communications can break down and the organization, as an entity, can lose its efficiency. In an attempt to overcome such problems, the "functional" organization was developed by those involved in management.

The functional organization also is in the form of a pyramid, with each of the functions required for the organization to achieve its objectives performed by a group of specialists, one of whom serves as the leader. Examples of such functional groups within a business organization are a financial group, a research and development group, a marketing group, and a production group. Such functional organizations work well when there is good coordination and communication among the various groups. However, if jealousies develop and communications break down, the organization can have problems. A functional group, for example, may act as an entity in itself without regard for the activities of, or the need for interaction with, other functional groups. If functional groups are separated geographically, communications become more difficult, and provincial attitudes may develop within one or several of the groups.

In an attempt to overcome some of the problems of functional management structures, another form of organization, called the "matrix" organization, has been developed. The primary characteristic of the matrix organization is that an individual working within it may have two bosses. In a consulting engineering firm, one of the engineer's supervisors is the senior person within the functional group. The other supervisor is the project manager to whom the engineer is assigned. Both supervisors have line authority over the individual, one in relation to the project and the other in relation to the engineer's disciplinary function as a mechanical, electrical, structural, or other type of engineer.

The matrix organization is a deviation from the traditional one-worker–one-boss relationship. People normally feel more secure with one supervisor whom they know and understand than with two. Hence, there can be problems within the matrix organization as well as within the other kinds of organization.

What does this discussion of organization mean in connection with the consulting engineering business? In the initial stages of the life of a consulting engineering firm, a simple pyramid organization may be satisfactory and efficient. As the business expands and projects become more complex, it is probable that functional groups will be needed. In fact, these functional groups may evolve through needs that develop in the firm, rather than through conscious decisions on the part of the firm's managers to move into a functional organization. Obviously, accounting is a necessary function for all businesses. As a business grows, the accounting needs of the business increase. Management of accounts receivable, cash flow, financing, preparation of tax returns, payment of accounts payable, and payroll preparation all must be handled if the business is to be viable. Thus, an accounting department (or functional group) evolves, or is formally established, within the firm to handle these matters. A personnel department is formed in much the same manner, although it may develop at a slower pace than the accounting group. In the engineering work performed by the firm, functional groups also evolve or are consciously established. If a firm started by providing consulting services in one discipline, such as mechanical engineering, it might subsequently expand and add civil engineering, electrical engineering, and architectural services. Each of these services would become a functional group within the organization. Marketing and research and development similarly become functional groups.

There is no one type of organization that is best for all consulting engineering firms. Each firm must adopt an organizational structure that fulfills its needs at specific times in its life and growth.

Management

The managers of a consulting engineering business are managers of a people business. People are the producers of the end product, and the quality of the product is dependent on the technical skills, imagination, and ingenuity of the people who produce the product.

The managers must understand the people who are working for the firm: their goals and objectives and the things that motivate them to perform in a superior manner. The goals and objectives of the firm must be consistent with the personal goals and objectives of the people within the firm. Managers must make short-, medium-, and long-range plans for the firm, and they must make immediate plans for handling its specific projects. They must provide the staffing for projects and decide if the overall staff is sufficient for future work. In addition, managers must establish systems of controls to evaluate progress being made toward achieving the firm's goals and objectives, and systems to determine if individual projects are being performed on schedule and within budget. Thus, management has the functions of planning, organizing, directing, staffing, and controlling for the firm as a whole and for the projects performed by the firm. Management also has the responsibility for marketing the firm's services.

In regard to personnel, management has the responsibilities to provide (1) a working environment that is satisfying to the people involved, (2) the leadership to develop people's confidence that their careers in the firm will be rewarding, (3) the incentives to motivate people to perform to the best of their abilities, and (4) a reasonable profit so the firm and the people in it can survive and prosper.

Is there a conflict between the need for a consulting engineering organization to make a profit and the professional responsibility of the engineers to provide quality engineering? The answer is "no." Consulting engineers have the responsibility of providing their clients with engineered products, whether they are designs and specifications or reports containing recommendations that will meet the clients' needs and protect the health, safety, and welfare of the general public. When the consulting engineer provides the client with engineering services that fulfill the client's needs in a safe and satisfactory manner within budget, the engineer has fulfilled his obligations. The engineer is required to perform the design work within the standards of the profession. If the client imposes budgetary restraints that might result in dangerous or unsafe conditions, the engineer is obliged to make this known to his client and to refuse to sign or seal any documents pertaining to such engineering work.

Problems can develop within a consulting engineering organization if the obligations of the organization are not fully communicated to all personnel. Groups or individuals may feel that everything produced must be the epitome of quality. If, in striving to achieve such quality, the engineers ignore time and budgets, the firm will encounter economic difficulties. Clients do not like to pay for overruns unless they are convinced in advance that such overruns are necessary and beneficial to their projects.

Engineers and consulting engineering firms want to build and maintain a reputation for providing engineering work of high quality. In fact, the success of a consulting engineering business is dependent on building and maintaining such a reputation. However, the consulting engineer also must consider the economics of the services he provides to his client.

Managers of consulting engineering firms must know how to manage professional personnel. In recent years, psychologists and others in the behavioral sciences have developed data that indicate that engineers and scientists obtain the most satisfaction from challenging technical work; they hope to be respected by their peers for the quality of the work they perform; and they enjoy working on and solving problems which are at the leading edge of the state of the art.

It has been found that money is not necessarily a strong motivating force toward better performance. This is not to imply that engineers and scientists are immune to the benefits attainable from money; they must have sufficient money to accommodate their basic needs of food, clothing, and shelter and to provide their families with a comfortable life. To some extent, money is a symbol of progress within one's profession and a measure of accomplishment in relation to one's peers. It is usually the symbolic aspect of financial reward that is important to engineers and scientists, not the material things that money can buy.

Performance Reviews

One of the difficult tasks faced by engineering managers is evaluating the performance of engineers who are under their supervision. It is an important task but one that many engineering managers do not perform as well as they should.

Some organizations have annual performance reviews, some have semiannual reviews, others have ongoing reviews, and some organizations have no reviews at all. Usually, performance reviews are associated with salary reviews, and when so related, they take on an added significance. The problems people have during performance reviews basically are problems of communication. The manager may have formed expectations regarding the engineer's performance but failed to communicate them to the individual in advance. When performance review time arrives, the reviewer may stress the negative aspects of the engineer's performance in areas the engineer did not know were important. This is unfair, and if the performance review process does not bring about improved performance on the part of the individual who is being reviewed, the fault lies with the reviewer.

Engineering managers can solve this kind of problem by developing sets of specific objectives to be accomplished by each individual under their supervision. These objectives should be discussed with the individual, agreement reached on which objectives can be achieved, and the achievable objectives placed in the individual's personal file. The manager should make an effort to have interim discussions with the individual to check on what progress is being made. This procedure makes it easier for the manager and the individuals being reviewed to communicate with each other since they have specific objectives to discuss that both have agreed are attainable.

In conducting performance reviews, the reviewer must be careful to maintain his objectivity and not be influenced by the personalities of the people being reviewed or by personal relationships. The reviewer should not try to practice amateur psychology. The reviewer's function is to evaluate the contributions each person has made to the organization, to provide guidance and motivation to improve performance, and to develop within each individual a sense that personal goals and ambitions are in harmony with the goals and objectives of the firm.

Continuing Education

In managing consulting engineering businesses, the managers must be constantly aware of the need to maintain and enhance the technical and professional capabilities of the members of the organization. It is part of management's function to encourage, assist, and even demand that members participate in continuing education programs, seminars, and home-study activities to keep abreast of the latest developments in their fields of expertise. Management must be prepared to pay a portion or all of the costs associated with such activities. For the success of the organization, it is necessary that the engineering personnel be knowledgeable about the latest developments in their field.

Planning

There are two major aspects of planning in a consulting engineering firm. The first is planning for the firm as a whole, and the second is planning for specific projects in which the firm is engaged. In planning for the firm as a whole, both short- and long-range plans are needed. Short-range plans might be those which the firm expects to accomplish within 1 year; long-range plans might be those the firm wishes to accomplish in 3, 5, or even 10 years. Obviously, the longer the time span, the less specific the plan can be.

In developing a one-year plan, managers use the data from their previous year's performance. An income and expense report for the forthcoming year can be established based on the preceding year's performance with certain adjustments for anticipated inflation and escalation of salaries. Such an income and expense report can then be used as a guideline in checking the actual figures that develop during the forthcoming year. If there are major deviations as the actual figures are developed, management must act to revise its plans to accommodate the unanticipated situation. If business volume is greater than planned, management must hire additional personnel to perform the greater volume of work.

There is a time lag between the start of hiring and the integration of new personnel into the work force. During this time lag, work must be accomplished and the clients' deadlines met. This may require overtime work by existing personnel, which can create personnel and morale problems. Additional office space may be needed but not be readily available. Required technical specialists may not be available at all.

Of course, the engineering manager should have been wise enough to have anticipated the increased volume and to have planned accordingly. However, had the manager planned for an increased volume of business that did not materialize, he would be faulted for overoptimism and for wasting the firm's resources. Planning is precarious, particularly in the consulting engineering business, as the business can fluctuate substantially from year to year due to external forces over which the engineering manager has no control.

Rather than merely extrapolating from preceding years' figures, it behooves the engineering manager to evaluate the external conditions that may affect the business and to develop an income and expense report that reflects the best available judgment on prospective business and the people and facilities required to do that business. The prognostications may be wrong; however, they generally will be better than an extrapolation of the previous year's results or no plan at all. In connection with the development of the numerical plan, the manager must provide for a regular comparison of the plan with actual results so that action can be taken when deviations occur.

In addition to a numerical plan, the consulting engineering

manager should describe the thinking which was used in developing the plan, including anticipation of business sources, projection of marketing strategies to obtain business, anticipation of personnel requirements, and other things that need to be done to achieve the planned results.

In planning for 3, 5, or 10 years ahead, the plans should be less specific numerically, but should contain descriptions of goals and objectives, strategies for achieving them, and the methods to be used to implement the strategies.

Planning for a specific project in a consulting engineering firm often starts when the firm is called upon by a client or potential client to make a proposal presentation regarding the firm's capabilities to undertake a specific assignment. If the firm is eager to obtain the assignment, the managers must prepare and plan the presentation in such a way that the client is impressed with the credentials of the firm and the manner in which the firm will handle the project. Clients who purchase engineering services are interested in the technical capability of the people who will be working on their project, the management capability to complete a project on time and within budget, and the overall resources of a firm to handle their project. In preparing for a presentation to a client, it is necessary to plan the way in which the firm will perform the project and to communicate the plan in an effective manner to the client. At the presentation stage, the engineering firm may have only sketchy information regarding the project and the client's needs. Hence, it is difficult to make detailed plans for the presentation due to lack of information.

More detailed planning is required when the consulting engineering firm is asked by a client to prepare a formal proposal. Requests for proposals (RFPs) may be very detailed and specific or they may be very general and conceptual, leaving the details to the consulting engineer. In developing a proposal, the consulting engineer must determine the engineering capabilities required; estimate the hours required for each; and take into account such variables as support staff required, computer usage, and field visits. As part of the proposal, the consulting engineer may be asked to identify specific individuals for technical and managerial positions and essentially guarantee that those individuals will be available for the project if and when it is authorized.

Usually, a project is dependent at various stages on input from the client or others. It is important to recognize these needs during the preparation of the proposal and to emphasize that such information must be provided in a timely manner if the project is to be completed within the desired schedule and budget.

When the proposal has been accepted and the project authorized, the planning process used in the proposal preparation stage must be fine-tuned. Individuals in the organization are selected and committed to the project. The project is broken into elements and responsibilities assigned to individuals who will supervise and do the engineering work. Specific schedules and budgets are developed for each element. In major engineering projects, the elements of work often are interdependent; i.e., one element cannot be started until others have been completed or have progressed substantially toward completion. Such interdependence must be recognized in the scheduling of the project. If the engineering project is complex, it may be beneficial to use a critical path method (CPM) or similar technique in developing the schedule.

Managing the Project

After the plans for the project have been developed, the project manager has the responsibility of controlling the project so that it is completed in accordance with the plan. One of the first steps is to meet with the key personnel who are to be involved in the project and make sure that all understand their roles. It is most helpful if these key personnel are involved in the planning stages of the project and participate in the development of budgets and schedules.

In controlling a project, the managers must have timely data on the expenditures to date for each of the elements and the relationship between the expenditures and the percent of completion. These are compared with the original plan to determine if the project is on schedule and within budget. The employees and principals in most offices record time spent on various projects on which they work. These data can be sorted out by computer or by hand and recorded for each project on which the firm is working. The data can be further divided into elements for each project through coding and then passed on to project managers to provide them with the expenditures to date. The data on percent completion of each of the elements in a project are not as easily obtained as the data on expenditures. In a design project, if each of the elements has an estimated number of drawings, the number of drawings completed in relation to the estimated total can be used as a basis for percent of completion. For projects in which drawings are not a sufficient guideline, the manager working on each of the elements must make periodic estimates of the percent completion and pass on these estimates to the project manager. During a project the client may request that changes be made from the concepts initially agreed upon. In other instances, the consulting engineer may recommend certain changes that would be beneficial to the project. Such changes must be thoroughly discussed with the client, and understandings must be reached on the effects on the time schedule and budget. The changes then can be incorporated in the overall plan and schedule.

A successful project for a consulting engineering firm is one that is completed on time and within budget, and that satisfies the needs and expectations of the client.

THE MARKETING OF CONSULTING ENGINEERING SERVICES

Edward K. Bryant

Partner (Retired), Tippetts-Abbett-McCarthy-Stratton

Scope of Work

As long as there are people in the world who crave social and economic progress, there will be a market for consulting engineers. The engineer in private practice is not only a designer, but also a motivator who identifies needs, forecasts change, and induces and influences development. By the very nature of his calling, the consulting engineer creates a market for his services.

The basic reason for engaging consultants is to accelerate the application of technical, economic, and managerial skills to the solution of practical problems. These may be the installation of facilities, the application of new technology, the utilization of resources, the development of skills, or the adoption of new managerial procedures and methodology. Because of the urgent need in developing countries for speeding socioeconomic development, it is particularly important that those nations take full advantage of the knowledge, expertise, and experience that have evolved in mature economies.

The major reasons for the use of consultants by private establishments, industrial associations, institutions, and government agencies are:

1. To shorten the time involved in obtaining the necessary background, experience, and judgment required to establish new operations or procedures
2. To secure independent, objective analyses and recommendations

regarding plans for undertakings, and to confirm their feasibility before they are activated

3. To supplement internal staffs of specialized personnel to handle excessive workloads
4. To obtain fresh points of view so that alternative courses of action are considered before decisions are made
5. To design and carry out training programs for internal personnel, either as separate projects or as on-the-job training

The types of assistance offered by consultants may be classified in six main groups:

1. Engineering projects, such as transportation, communications, utilities, and miscellaneous structures
2. Agricultural and irrigation projects
3. Industrial projects, such as the adaptation of technology to product and process development
4. Managerial studies, including organizational patterns, operating policies, and personnel management
5. Economic analyses, including feasibility, marketing, and financial investigations
6. Training programs, including preparation of material and conducting of courses at various organizational levels

It is a misconception that consultants to industrial organizations in mature economies serve mostly small establishments that lack their own specialized personnel. On the contrary, the large- and medium-sized organizations and agencies seeking to supplement their internal resources or skills are the major source of consulting assignments.

Job Identification

To establish his place in industrialized countries, the consultant must demonstrate his ability to assist organizations in improving their operating and managerial postures in their own locations. In doing this, the consultant is obliged to act in the best interest of his client, and to this end he operates as an extension of the client's own staff. That relationship must be adopted by the client as well. Without this community of goals, interests, and objectives, the progress of any consulting project is severely handicapped. The establishment of this spirit of cooperation and sympathetic understanding is especially important in developing countries to overcome difficulties that may arise from the differences in the cultural backgrounds of client and consultant.

Consultants' talents provide a reservoir of knowledge, skills, and experience available to government agencies undertaking public improvement and industrial development. Such services are especially important in decreasing the time required to initiate new undertakings by making available the information necessary for rapid implementation of plans. Through the use of consultants, organizations in developing countries can acquire the specialized background needed to supplement their own more limited cadres of trained workers. If they are to use this external resource successfully, they must understand the types of assistance available, the conditions under which they may be obtained, and the relationships necessary to ensure optimum benefits.

An older firm may be able to operate successfully with repeat assignments from an established clientele that has been served satisfactorily over a long period of time, while it also seeks to add other commissions. The younger firm may be fortunate enough to be invited to propose for work and to undertake an assignment. More likely, however, it will have to anticipate job opportunities, promote implementation of improvement and development projects, possibly form an alliance with another firm of engineers or architects to perform a portion of a job, or undertake a joint venture with a construction contractor on a turnkey project.

One of the more satisfactory and rewarding methods of getting business is to establish a good reputation with government agencies, funding institutions, and industrial development companies that may lead to consideration for further commissions or, at least, requests for proposals for new work.

Other opportunities are sometimes offered by invitations to participate in a joint venture with an architect, economist, local consultant, or another engineer who may already have obtained a commitment for a study or project work. This approach is somewhat different from that of a joint venture or consortium formed to compete with other American firms, joint ventures, or consortia. It also differs from an association with an agent who acts as entrepreneur or broker, an arrangement which, to many professional firms, is of questionable ethics and value.

Local newspapers (particularly those with broad business and international coverage), technical magazines, commercial journals, and information services are acknowledged sources of leads on potential work. Articles describing an ongoing survey or economical engineering study can be an indicator of future investigations, design, and construction.

Response to advertised needs of government agencies, public works departments, public utilities, and international funding agencies for consulting services can sometimes lead to professional contracts. Basic marketing techniques are applicable to both public and private clients. The main need in obtaining assignments is for the consultant to be alert to any and all job opportunities and to make every effort to contact potential clients, selling them on the technical competence of the firm and ultimately negotiating a mutually satisfactory contract.

In respect to foreign work, the U.S. Agency for International Development (AID) projects are advertised in the *Commerce Business Daily* (U.S. Department of Commerce) well in advance of invitations for expressions of interest or proposals. The World Bank, the Inter-American Development Bank, and the Asian Development Bank all have monthly bulletins on forthcoming or ongoing work. In fact, the World Bank and AID mail out news releases almost daily on loans and credits for development projects. The United Nations *Pre-investment News,* which is published monthly, contains general information about projects, but the principal sources of information on UN and United Nations Development Programme (UNDP) projects are the Country Programmes prepared in each country under the general direction of the regional representative of the UNDP. Many other engineering and construction journals are valuable sources of information.* Careful review and analysis of media items such as these can be very productive; however, timeliness is essential.

Information garnered from publications should be supplemented

---

*For data and statistics of developing countries, lists of international funding agencies and U.S. government agencies concerned with foreign activities of interest to consulting engineers, refer to *The International Consultant* by H. Peter Guttmann (McGraw-Hill, New York, 1976).

by personal calls on government officials, department heads (e.g., highways, water supply and waste disposal, electricity and gas supply), engineers, economists, and mission members at the headquarters of an agency. Similarly, private industry is a fertile market to cultivate. Of considerable value are calls on agents and representatives of foreign governments. This is particularly true in foreign countries, where visits to government agencies may reveal project plans and sometimes involve informal consultation and advice leading to more substantial involvement.

Calls on local consulting firms in a foreign country may be well worthwhile in developing a future association in which the local firm performs a portion of the work, providing local personnel and support facilities and assisting in expediting paper processing through local government offices. The local firm frequently brings in up-to-date news of potential work, obtains introductions to government officials, and helps in other ways in bringing in new business.

"Missionary work" of this type is a major producer of new work, and the U.S. Foreign Service personnel stationed abroad can play a large role in providing intelligence to consultants and introductions to appropriate officials of public agencies and private organizations. They also can promote or intervene on behalf of U.S. firms during proposal evaluation and consultant selection stages. Their assistance during preparation of the proposal can prove invaluable with their detailed knowledge of local conditions; the availability of local consultants and expert staff; local laws, customs, and business practices; taxes, social benefits, and hiring procedures for local employees; as well as government practices in respect to such things as letters of credit, income taxes, and customs duty.

In some parts of the world an agent is stipulated by the client. Like the local consulting firm, he can be very helpful in providing information and arranging introductions to potential clients. However, there may be drawbacks to employment of agents recommended by the client.

Marketing

Consultants seeking private work with an industry or a utility such as a power corporation, a railroad, or a water company frequently obtain assignments on the basis of the firm's experience record, the client's previous experience with the firm and the personal knowledge of a principal, or a good reference from a colleague.

In addition to personal calls on principals of prospective clients with a view toward being considered for assignments, consultants often prepare comprehensive brochures outlining their capabilities and experience. Included in the brochures are detailed professional curricula vitae of the principals of the firm and the key personnel and descriptions of projects of different types on which the firm has been engaged.

Most public agencies have a registration form which provides detailed information on consulting firms. The *Consulting Firm Registration Form* (Figure 5–1), recommended by the International Federation of Consulting Engineers (FIDIC) may be used by the agency as a basis for formulating a "long list" of consultants being considered.

Competition

In selecting a consulting firm, private companies generally will inquire about similar work performed by the consultant and will check references. Seldom do private clients in foreign countries require anything further except information as to who will be the firm's representative handling the job at the site. The reputation of the firm is of prime importance with private clients, but one's connections may be the determining factor in the final selection. Cost also may be a major consideration with foreign private clients.

In the private sector, competition derives largely from local engineering firms. Outside of the United States and Great Britain, there are few large, independent consulting firms, although there are independent firms in all of the 35 countries represented in FIDIC. Most engineers in other foreign countries have been associated with contractors or government agencies, and large engineering projects have generally been handled on a turnkey basis. This practice has extended to the OPEC countries in the middle east and north Africa although it is more prevalent in private work than in public. Foreign industry, with its eye on the more obvious construction costs, is inclined toward the package job, and U.S. firms sometimes have been successful in breaking into this field, particularly in a specialized line. However, in a recent edition of the UNESCO manual for the use of consultants, it is pointed out that when a project is designed and constructed as a package job, "there is a conflict of interest on the contractor's part which does not insure the client of unbiased engineering advice or complete integrity in performance of the construction work."

For foreign contracts, competition among U.S. firms is, of course, stiffest on U.S. government–sponsored projects. On projects sponsored by the World Bank, foreign firms frequently are selected because of the international nature of the Bank. Foreign countries are inclined to select their own nationals when qualified firms are available. The newer countries often go to their traditional consultants, firms located in the countries of which the new nations were formerly colonies. Occasionally, however, they will assert their independence by going elsewhere.

Paying commissions or affording other means of financial benefits to government officials is accepted as commonplace in certain countries. This obviously presents problems, since reputable U.S. professional service firms consider the practice dishonest and shun it. In at least two countries, the heads of state overtly permit their ministers and high officials to "share" in contract fees in the belief that a hitherto nonexistent middle class will be created, spreading the purchasing base and thus assisting in the overall economic expansion of the country. Some officials of foreign governments have expressed surprise and chagrin at the adverse attitude with which U.S. engineers view this practice.

Other sources of stiff competition, particularly those funded by the U.S. government at home and abroad, are U.S. government public agencies such as the Army Corps of Engineers, the Bureau of Reclamation and the Federal Highway Administration. On the other hand, the Corps of Engineers claims that its job overseas is to make a place for U.S. designers and contractors. Foreign government agencies also are strong competitors for consulting work at home and abroad, particularly in specialized fields such as airports, railroads, dams, and testing laboratories.

Among the major competitors for U.S. firms to overcome abroad are consortia of foreign consultants promoted by, and in many instances subsidized by, their governments. These consortia often receive favorable tax exemptions, allowances for promotional costs,

Agency:

Consulting Firm Registration Form

Date (Month, Day, Year)

1. **Firm Name** (firm to be registered)	Year Estab.	State or Country	Type of Organization			
			Indiv.	Partshp.	Corp.	Other

1a. Affiliated Firms

2. **Home Office(s) Business Address(es)**, Telephone No., Cable Address, Telex No. Officers or Partners to be contacted

3. **Former Firm Name(s), if any, and year established**	4. **Firm ownership**

5. **Present Branch Office(s) and year established** Address, Telephone No., Cable Address, Telex No., Person in Charge

6. **Number of personnel in your present organization(s) listed in 1 and 1a**

Architects	Civil and Structural Engineers	Electrical Engineers	Mechanical Engineers	Construction Management	Economists	Operations & Management Specialists	Others (Specify)	Others (Specify)

Surveyors	Estimators	Inspectors	Technicians & Draftsmen	Administration and Clerical	Specification Writers	Others (Specify)	Others (Specify)	Total

7. **Annual volume of gross fees (last 5 years) in US $ (per 1 and 1a)** — Financial rating or bank reference

	Prime Consulting Firm	Associate and Joint Venture	Total
19	$		
19	$		
19	$		
19	$		
19	$		
		Total	

8. **Largest projects handled by firm as prime consultant in major fields only**
Show name of project, type of service, client reference and engineer's level of effort
Level of effort to be classified as follows:
Class 1 - Fee less than US $ 100,000 or 20 man months.
Class 2 - Fee from US $ 100,000 to US $ 500,000 or from 20 man months to 100 man months
Class 3 - Fee from US $ 500,000 to US $ 1,000,000 or from 100 man months to 200 man months
Class 4 - Fee over US $ 1,000,000 or over 200 man months

9. **Partners, directors, officers, and key personnel of firm**

Name and Title	Degree(s)	Years with Firm	Year of Birth

Figure 5–1(a)

Figure 5–1(a-d) Consulting firm registration form recommended by the International Federation of Consulting Engineers (FIDIC).

10. Fields of specialization of permanent full-time staff (Check Appropriate Items)

A	Agricultural and natural resources	C	Public utilities and related fields (continued)	D	Industry (continued)
					D-21 Steel and Iron Works
	A-1 Farm Mechanization		C-9 Housing		D-22 Textiles
	A-2 Field and Horticultural Crops		C-10 Industrial Utilities		D-23 Timber Processing
	A-3 Fisheries		C-11 Marina Terminal Facilities		Others (Specify)
	A-4 Forestry and Forest Products		C-12 Mining		D-24
	A-5 Irrigation and Flood Control		C-13 Nuclear Energy		D-25
	A-6 Land and Water Feasibility Studies		C-14 Parking Facilities	E	Architecture and related fields
			C-15 Power Stations		
	A-7 Land Reclamation and Soil Conservation		C-16 Power Transmission and Distribution		E-1 Conservation
					E-2 Educational Facilities
	A-8 Livestock		C-17 Solid Waste Management		E-3 Factories and Buildings
	A-9 Marketing and Credit		C-18 Buildings		E-4 Parks
	A-10 River Regulation and Control		C-19 Telecommunications		E-5 Social and Low Cost Housing
	A-11 Storage Facilities		C-20 Wastewater Collection, Treatment and Disposal		E-6 Urban Development and City Planning
	Others (Specify)				
	A-12		C-21 Water Supply and Distribution		E-7 Zoos
	A-13		Others (Specify)		Others (Specify)
	A-14		C-22		E-8
B	Transport		C-23		E-9
	B-1 Airports and Air Transport		C-24	F	Economic planning and related fields
	B-2 Bridges		C-25		
	B-3 Bus Transport Facilities		C-26		F-1 Accounting and Auditing
	B-4 Highways and Road Transport		C-27		F-2 Economic Impact Statements
	B-5 Pipelines	D	Industry		F-3 Economic Policy
	B-6 Public Transport		D-1 Agricultural Products and Food Processing		F-4 Energy Conservation
	B-7 Rapid Transit				F-5 Finance
	B-8 Railroads		D-2 Bricks and Tiles		F-6 Foreign Trade
	B-9 River and Sea Transport		D-3 Cement Works		F-7 Marketing
	B-10 River-, Seaports and Harbors		D-4 Ceramics		F-8 Organization and Management of Public and/or Private Enterprises
	B-11 Subways		D-5 Chemical Plants (including Petrochemicals, Fertilisers, Plastics)		
	B-12 Tunnels				F-9 Regional Development Planning
	Others (Specify)		D-6 Coal		Others (Specify)
	B-13		D-7 Fish Processing		F-10
	B-14		D-8 Foundries	G	Tourism
	B-15		D-9 Glass Plants		G-1 Hotel Development
C	Public utilities and related fields		D-10 Hides and Leather Processing		G-2 Resort Development
			D-11 Industrial Estates		Others (Specify)
	C-1 Air Pollution Control		D-12 Machinery Plants		G-3
	C-2 Cartography		D-13 Materials Handling		G-4
	C-3 Dams		D-14 Metallurgical		
	C-4 Drainage		D-15 Mineralogy		
	C-5 Electrical Installations		D-16 Non-ferrous Processing Plants		
	C-6 Gas Installations and Transmissions		D-17 Oil		
			D-18 Pharmaceutical Plants		
	C-7 Heating, Ventilating, Air-Conditioning		D-19 Pulp and Paper		
			D-20 Rubber		
	C-8 Hospitals				

Date   Name of Firm   Page 4 of 7

Figure 5–1(b)

11. Types of services

A.	Advisory Services	W.	Planning Studies
B.	Aerial Photography	X.	Project Management
C.	Architectural	Y.	Purchasing, Inspection and Testing of Materials and Equipment
D.	Computer Services		
E.	Construction Management	Z.	Resources Surveys
F.	Design of Machinery and Equipment	Z-1	Rate Studies and Appraisals
G.	Economic Studies	Z-2	Sector Studies
H.	Engineering Design, Estimating, Preparation of Contract Documents, Bid Evaluation	Z-3	Soils Engineering, Foundation Engineering & Design
		Z-4	Supervision of Construction or Equipment Installation Contracts
I.	Environmental Studies		
J.	Farm Extension Services	Z-5	Testing and Inspection
K.	Geological Surveys	Z-6	Topographical and Soil Surveys
L.	Geophysical Surveys	Z-7	Technical Feasibility Studies and Preliminary Engineering
M.	Hydro-Geology		
N.	Hydrological Surveys	Z-8	Traffic Studies
O.	Industrial Process Engineering	Z-9	Value Analysis
P.	Machine Processing of Engineering Data		Others (Specify)
Q.	Management Studies	Z-10	
R.	Market Surveys	Z-11	
S.	Mineral Surveys, Photo Interpretation	Z-12	
T.	Mineral Exploration	Z-13	
U.	Oceanography	Z-14	
V.	Operation and Maintenance	Z-15	

12. Countries in which work performed within past 10 years (Check Appropriate Countries)

Afghanistan	Equatorial Guinea	Lesotho	Sierra Leone
Albania	Ethiopia	Liberia	Singapore
Algeria	Fiji	Libya	Somali (Dem. Rep. of)
Argentina	Finland	Liechtenstein	South Africa
Australia	France	Luxembourg	Spain
Austria	Gabon	Madagascar	Sri Lanka (Ceylon)
Bahamas	Gambia (The)	Malawi	Sudan
Bahrain	Germany (Dem. Rep. of)	Malaysia	Swaziland
Bangladesh	Germany (Fed. Rep. of)	Maldives	Sweden
Barbados	Ghana	Mali	Switzerland
Belgium	Greece	Malta	Syria
Benin (Dahomey)	Grenada	Mauritania	Tanzania
Bhutan	Guatemala	Mauritius	Thailand
Bolivia	Guinea	Mexico	Togo
Botswana	Guinea-Bissau	Monaco	Trinidad and Tobago
Brazil	Guyana	Mongolia	Tunisia
Bulgaria	Haiti	Morocco	Turkey
Burma	Holy See	Nepal	Uganda
Burundi	Honduras	Netherlands	Ukrainian SSR
Byelorussian SSR	Hungary	New Zealand	USSR
Cameroon	Iceland	Nicaragua	United Arab Emirates
Canada	India	Niger	United Kingdom
Central African Rep.	Indonesia	Nigeria	United States
Chad	Iran	Norway	Upper Volta
Chile	Iraq	Oman	Uruguay
China	Ireland	Pakistan	Venezuela
Colombia	Israel	Panama	Vietnam (Rep. of)
Congo (People's Rep. of)	Italy	Paraguay	Western Samoa
Costa Rica	Ivory Coast	Peru	Yemen (Aden)
Cuba	Jamaica	Philippines	Yemen (Sanaa)
Cyprus	Japan	Poland	Yugoslavia
Czechoslovakia	Jordan (The Hashemite Kingdom of)	Portugal	Zaire
Denmark	Kenya	Qatar	Zambia
Dominican Rep.	Korea (Republic of)	Romania	
Ecuador	Kuwait	Rwanda	Others (Specify)
Egypt	Khymer Republic (Cambodia)	San Marino	
El Salvador	Laos	Saudi Arabia	
	Lebanon	Senegal	

Date   Name of Firm

Figure 5-1(c)

13. Narrative Description of firm

(continue on additional page if necessary)

As of this date   the foregoing is a true statement of facts.

Name of firm submitting questionnaire

Typed name and title of person signing   Signature

14. Typical projects for which consultant services have been furnished during past five years

(Reference sheets may be submitted for as many projects as desired. Sheets should include at least one project in each field of specialization checked in Item 10 and each type of service checked in Item 11).

Name of overall project

Location of overall project

Engineers level of effort
(For classifications see Section 8)
Owner's name and address

Year firm's services completed (indicate if estimated or actual)

Associated firms

Description of project

(firm may submit as many pages as necessary)

Description of services firm provided

List all fields of experience (by symbols from Item 10) for associated aspects of overall project

List all types of services (by symbols from Item 11) for associated aspects of overall project

Figure 5–1(d)

and other assistance to lessen overhead costs, and they are frequently promoted by the embassy staff in the host country. When such a consortium of consultants is retained, the way is paved for award of contracts to construction firms of the sponsoring country and for sale of their manufactured supplies and equipment. In still other cases, it is a form of technical assistance, or a subsidy. United States antitrust laws relative to cartels limit the extent to which U.S. consultants can organize and participate in such consortia.

Another form of competition at home and abroad is the utilization of individual experts, pickup teams of experts, universities, not-for-profit foundations, and government agencies. In defense of private consulting firms, Paul Hoffman, the administrator of UNDP for many years, stated: "The use of qualified consulting services on a subcontract basis offers important advantages in the execution of many UNDP-assisted projects." He pointed out that "private firms can furnish an experienced team that is used to working together and is effectively directed and controlled, that has a strong home office backstop organization, that can schedule its staff to the field when, as, and if needed, and can frequently use them intermittently to the economy of the job." It was further pointed out that "a consultant firm is jealous of its reputation for competence and performance and accepts responsibility for the successful execution of a commission. It cannot afford to have failures if it intends to continue to practice." Furthermore, the use of a consultant firm ensures a continuity of interest and records for extensions of the original commission or a continuing service of advice on maintenance and operation. Hoffman also stated that:

The objective of feasibility studies is to lead to major capital expenditures of permanent benefit to the recipient country. We believe that the investing sources will normally prefer to do so based on the opinions of proven consultants rather than on those of individuals, however competent. Almost invariably further interrogation or supplementary studies are needed after the completion of the main feasibility stage but before capital investment starts. A consulting firm remains to prove this continuity, whereas teams of individuals normally disband upon completion. The absence of continuity, forcing perhaps complete reassessment, may be very costly and alone justify any apparent initial higher cost from the use of consultants.

With respect to differentials in costing, Hoffman emphasized that "the question of cost centers largely around that of overheads. Except for top coordinators and specialists, the salary of a recruited individual appears to be much lower but is in fact very considerable."

The advantages of consulting firms over universities, foundations, and government agencies are similar, though perhaps to a lesser degree. Nevertheless, the value of a feasibility report to the investment banker is far greater if it is prepared by a consultant firm than if by some agency that does not guarantee perpetuation of responsibility.

In some countries corporate and tax laws sometimes make it difficult for other than local firms to work on private foreign projects. Contracts with foreign governments generally contain a protective clause in these as well as other respects, but on a contract with a private company a consultant generally is subject to all the local laws which, when applied in a strange country, may be quite onerous. Income taxes may be a particularly high hurdle when sliding-scale rates originally established for relatively low local salaries are applied to foreigners' salaries plus allowances. In some countries, all of the firm's income, wherever earned, is subject to tax. This can virtually exclude a foreign firm from operating in that country. However, the practice of forming a special company for each project might circumvent such a situation.

Selection of Consultant (Long List)

The process of selecting a consultant varies between private and public clients, and even among various public agencies. The recommended and generally accepted procedure is:

- Define the project.
- Identify potential firms.
- Determine the firm best meeting the client's needs.
- Discuss the scope of the project with the firm.
- Negotiate the terms of the agreement and the price.

An initial step by the client in identifying a potential consultant may be reference to specialized directories of firms prepared by professional associations such as American Consulting Engineers Council (ACEC) and FIDIC. The ACEC Directory is limited to U.S. member firms, while the FIDIC Directory covers firms from its 35 or more member associations around the world. In these directories two pages are allotted to each subscribing firm, usually providing information on geographic areas of operation, organization and names of principals, a brief history, a list of types of services offered and the fields of practice, and a description of a few typical projects on which it has been engaged. These directories generally are distributed to government and funding agencies, both domestic and foreign, which may be involved with the employment of consultants. Since many of the firms shown in the directories are concerned with international work, copies of the U.S. directories usually are sent to all U.S. embassies, where the commercial attaché advises foreign government agencies of the availability of U.S. consultants for prospective work. It also enables the Department of Commerce to inform qualified consultants of opportunities abroad.

In general, when an agency decides to proceed with a project, it will prepare the terms of reference for the consultants and on the basis of information gained from brochures, registration forms, and personal knowledge, will invite expressions of interest from a number of firms it considers qualified for the job. Upon receipt of responses to this invitation a selection committee of qualified staff concerned with the project will select a long list of perhaps 15 firms to make proposals for the work.

Selection of a long list is on a purely mechanical or computer basis, with little regard for known technical competence. The result is that good firms may not be considered or may be eliminated from consideration and poor firms may surface. Some institutions try to achieve a geographical spread in the selection of consultants for short lists. There also may be an attempt to eliminate firms that have appeared on previous selection lists or have had other work with the agencies. The net result of this discrimination is that consultants find it desirable to respond to a great number of notifications and requests for expressions of interest in order to be successful in obtaining one assignment. Obviously, this can be a rather expensive procedure. The expense is also increased when the invitation stipulates that a site visit must be made or attendance at a briefing session at some remote place is a requisite to the client's consideration of a proposal.

Consultants appreciate the necessity for these exercises but feel that the number of firms invited to perform them for each project should be kept to a minimum, perhaps three to five firms. In any event, the cost of preparing the proposal is included in the firm's overhead, which the client must bear in the long run.

Presentations

Following selection by the client of a long list of possible consultants, an opportunity is generally given to the consultants to make a presentation to the selection committee. The proposal is to provide information on the professional competence of the firm to perform the work, the availability and adequacy of staff, and its fiscal responsibility.

Usually the firm prepares a special brochure containing information applicable to the project. This would demonstrate its experience in the specific fields involved, listing similar projects and indicating their magnitude. It would also provide brief resumés of the staff to be assigned to the work. It probably would contain the firm's organization chart and a diagram or bar chart (PERT or CPM) indicating how it would proceed with the project. Frequently, large photographs, slides, or other visual aids are shown at the meeting to illustrate the firm's experience and competence.

Information on the firm would include a list of branch offices, indicating whether such offices are actually branches or are offices of associated firms or consultants. Emphasis may be put on the experience of the firm and staff in the specific geographic area of the project. In international work, language competence is important. Both familiarity with the area and ability to speak the native tongue are major factors in assessing firms competing for a particular job.

Information on the firm's financial rating is important when the magnitude of a project or the time lag in payments may require substantial financial resources. The list of jobs should show the largest jobs handled in various parts of the world.

During and after the formal presentation, members of the selection committee usually ask a number of questions, expanding on the information provided by the consultant. Obviously, it is important to be able to answer all questions in detail and to cover the entire field of possible inquiry. The consultant usually is expected to have three or more of its principals or staff present. A dry run of the presentation often is made by the consultant's representatives prior to the formal meeting in order to anticipate questions and prepare responses that will persuade the client of the firm's technical capability and its awareness of other possible methods of procedure.

If the terms of reference contain specific designs or specifications for the project, or detailed procedures for its execution, the consultant is given an opportunity during the presentation to suggest or recommend variations that he thinks might improve upon the execution of the contract or some of the elements of the end product. Such suggestions may be considered an indication of the proficiency of the consultant, his experience, or his innovative ability. There is more to getting a commission than merely being technically competent.

Proposals

Following the presentations by the consultants, the client's selection committee compiles a "short list" of possibly five consultants considered most suitable for the job. Proposals are invited from each of those firms.

Proposals generally are required to be made on a form prepared by the client in accordance with the terms of reference for the consultant's procedure. These are intended to disclose the extent of the following qualifications:

1. The consultant's background and experience in work of the kind involved
2. The consultant's experience in the client's geographic area
3. The consultant's work plan and staff organization to accomplish the work
4. Qualifications of the consultant's key personnel to be assigned to the work

If the decision is made to retain an independent, private firm of consultants, the selection of a firm to render engineering, economic, architectural, management, and other professional services should be made primarily upon the basis of qualifications. Quality, in terms of the consultant's ability to bring about practical, economical, and expeditious solutions to problems, is more important than cost. Competent professionals will not engage in cut-rate competition, but they are not inclined to overcharge. On the other hand, cheap advice is likely to be casual at best and often incompetent; consequently, it is usually more expensive in the end. Price competition for professional services most often results in the lowest price being offered by the firm which will provide the least service and which has the poorest qualifications. Sometimes it results in an underestimate of costs by a well-meaning but inexperienced firm, leading to later difficulty in carrying the work to completion.

Although the cost of professional services is of secondary importance, the fee for such services should be reasonable from the point of view of both the owner and the consultant. Certain recognized yardsticks are available for establishing the size of the fee. Most professional societies publish recommended fee schedules which are useful as a general guide. A careful analysis of the assignment, its complexity, the logistics involved in its accomplishment, and the time required or available for its completion will determine the direct cost of performing the services. The fee ordinarily is related only to the direct labor and administrative costs.

FIDIC, which is a federation of elected associations of consulting engineers representing the profession in their several countries, has formulated a procedure for selection of consulting engineers that has been widely adopted by government and financial agencies throughout the world.

Among major financial and funding agencies following this guideline are the International Bank for Reconstruction and Development (World Bank), the Inter-American Development Bank, the African Development Bank, the Asian Development Bank, the United Nations Development Programme, the World Health Organization, and, recently, the Food and Agriculture Organization.

It also is followed by major U.S. government agencies such as the Federal Highway Administration, Bureau of Reclamation, Army Corps of Engineers, Naval Facilities Engineering Command, and the Agency for International Development.

The FIDIC guide to the use of independent consultants states that:

The selection of a consulting engineer should never be based on competitive price bidding. Generally the amount of the fee paid to a consulting engineer is a minor consideration when compared to the total cost of a project. Any variation in fees charged by qualified consultants is a still smaller consideration. Therefore, differences in fees between consultants should not be given major consideration in the selection of the engineer. The degree of satisfactory completion of the project and the total cost will be greatly affected by the experience and skill of the engineer, his associates and staff and the amount of effort they put into the project. In order to obtain optimum results it is essential that the relationship between the client and the engineer be based on mutual confidence.

The reasons for objections to competitive bidding for engineering services by consulting engineers are not generally understood. There are many persons and organizations who feel that consulting engineers object to this practice solely for the protection of members of the profession. They see nothing wrong in obtaining engineering services in much the same manner that materials and equipment are purchased or contracts awarded. A little thought will show that there is no comparison between selling of goods and contracting on the one hand, and the provision of consulting engineering services on the other. Purchase agreements and contracts specifically limit the extent of the obligation of all parties. There are guarantees of quality and performance to protect the purchaser and owner. In these matters it is assumed that the supplier or contractor and the purchaser or owner are each acting in his own interest. The relationship between a consulting engineer and his client is entirely different. The service to be rendered cannot usually be completely defined. There is no protection to the client in the form of a guarantee. He is, therefore, dependent on the skill and integrity of the engineer to produce the best solution for him. As the engineer becomes the advisor and representative of the client, there should be no conflict of interests between the two. A consulting engineer must work in the best interests of his client, even at times to his own financial disadvantage. In engaging a consulting engineer for any purpose the client entrusts his interests to the judgement and integrity of the engineer. All this points to the necessity of keeping the relationship between client and consulting engineer on a highly ethical professional basis.

The policy manuals of many other professional engineering societies, government agencies, and funding institutions contain advice, instructions, and guidelines similar in most respects to the above.

Competitive Price Bidding

Advocates of competitive price bidding for engineering contracts, aside from thinking that the cheapest proposal is the most financially advantageous to them, believe that opportunity for corrupt practice is overcome, that time is saved in negotiations, and that contract administration problems are substantially reduced. In an effort to eliminate some of the criticism of priced proposals, requests are frequently made for two separate proposals. This method of selection is similar to selection by ability except that consulting engineers are requested to submit a priced proposal in two sealed envelopes. The first envelope contains the technical proposal exclusive of price; the second contains the proposed prices for the services. Normally these either consist of daily or monthly rates for various personnel levels.

The client or his advisory board will analyze the proposals and establish the order of merit, and contract negotiations will begin with the firm presenting the best proposal. The second envelope of this firm is opened in the presence of the firm, and the price information will then form the basis for contract negotiations. All other second envelopes should remain sealed, and if an agreement is reached with the first firm, the envelopes should be returned unopened to their respective firms.

If an agreement is not reached with the first firm, it should be advised by written notification. Negotiations then are undertaken with the second firm, and so on, until a satisfactory agreement is reached. Once a firm has been eliminated it should not be recalled for further negotiation.

In a variation of the two-envelope system the client opens the second envelopes of the two or three top-ranked consulting engineers at the same time in order to make an evaluation on a cost-weighted basis. That combines the merits of the technical proposals and the price.

The disadvantages and possible abuses of the two-envelope system are:

1. All the second envelopes can be opened by the client at the same time without the knowledge or the agreement of the consulting engineers. The consulting engineer with the lowest apparent price is invited for negotiations not knowing that he has been selected on price rather than ability. The client therefore takes

little or no account of the ability of the consulting engineer to complete the project.

2. The consulting engineer must set a price before discussions are held with the client about the scope of the consultant's work.
3. The consulting engineer may send in his prices in a way that conceals their true extent. This can be done by carefully relating the scope of the work with the price. Thus the client is lulled into a false sense of security. Sometimes, after the consulting engineer begins work, he points out that the scope of the project has changed and enters a higher price.

Consultants in general, and their professional associations, have taken a strong stand against the two-envelope system. Substantiating the professional stand against priced proposals, price being a major factor in the selection of an engineer, is legislation by the U.S. Congress known as the Brooks Law, which prohibits public agencies from receiving proposals based on price alone.

While this procedure, with variations in the rating of firms, is generally followed by clients for projects funded by international banks and funding agencies, other types of clients may have different procedures. For example, seldom, if ever, does one hear of a private businessperson requesting bids for engineering work from foreign engineers or even canvassing foreign engineers for estimates of their costs. They seem to appreciate that, as with other professional services, they will get what they pay for, and a low quotation for engineering work made in a price competition will, in all probability, get them minimal engineering from a firm struggling for existence among abler competitors. However, since they wish to take advantage of low costs, they almost always will employ local firms rather than foreign competitors of equal competence.

To qualify with foreign clients for work, other things being equal, a firm usually has to demonstrate its experience on projects or products of a like nature and magnitude. Frequently, an engineer is required to stipulate the specific staff members who will be assigned to the project. Sometimes a firm is asked to state what claims if any have been brought against it in the past by clients, and vice versa. Almost always, a financial statement is requested.

Evaluation of Proposals

The four major factors that are evaluated by such funding agencies in qualifying firms for contract negotiations are (1) experience of the firm on similar projects, (2) experience and ability of individual staff members to be assigned to the project, (3) reputation of the firm for satisfactory performance, (4) the firm's concept of the project work as indicated by its proposed procedure and estimated number of worker-months for accomplishment (too high or too low an estimation would reflect adversely on the firm's qualifications).

In general, on the date set forth in the invitation for submittal, all the proposals are exposed (in private) by the client, and each member of the selection committee evaluates every proposal in accordance with a previously developed rating system. A typical rating

Initial rating will be to assess the basic qualification of the proposer to do the job. The criteria will be rated as **Significant, Adequate, Marginal, Not Acceptable** or **Not Known**. **"Not Known"** means that there is no adverse information. A rating of **Not Acceptable** in any category will disqualify the proposer from further consideration. The proposer may be disqualified with a rating of **Marginal** in more than two areas. Any **Marginal** rating will be noted under Part III.

	S	A	M	NA	NK
1. Compliance with Terms of Reference					
2. Financial Stability					
3. Professional and ethical reputation					
4. Absence of potential conflict of interest					
5. Demonstrated experience of proposer in handling contracts of comparable size and complexity, including overseas experience					
6. Manageability and cohesion of consortium					
7. Majority of key staff from permanent staff of the consultant					
8. Experience in environmental evaluation					
9. Experience in (Type of Project under consideration)					
10. Experience in master planning (Type of Project)					
11. Experience in design of (Type of Project)					

Figure 5–2 Critieria by which the client can rate a consultant's basic qualifications.

system is shown in Figures 5-2 through 5-7. Comments on this form were among those made by Dr. Louis Berger, vice chairman of Louis Berger International, Inc., East Orange, N.J., at the FIDIC Seminar held in Teheran in April 1976*:

Figure 5–2: Indicated on Figure 5–2 are the criteria by which the client can rate a consultant's basic qualifications. The column designated NK (not known) means no adverse information. A rating of nonacceptable in any category should automatically disqualify the consultant from further consideration. Included within the basic qualifications are the consultant's financial capability with evidence of the company's growth within the last ten years. Obviously, the consultant must have adequate financial resources as related to the size of the contract. The consultant must also establish that his firm regularly engages in consulting work—thereby eliminating firms lacking the required expertise or experience. The consultant's statement of qualifications should indicate satisfactory performance on previous contracts. Another important item concerns staffing of the key personnel for the particular job. Are they members of the permanent staff of the consultant? Or are they all brought in from outside to accomplish the task? Permanent staff personnel are imperative for senior posts.

Figure 5–3. Detailed qualification statements for the specific type of project envisaged must be submitted in order for the client to evaluate the expertise and experience of the proposer. Each item indicated on the diagram must be covered adequately—either by the written technological submission, or through oral interview.

Figure 5–4. The approach and work plan. The client expects the consultant to demonstrate that he thoroughly understands the problem and has developed a project overview. In this detailed workplan, the consultant must present his evaluation of critical areas and discuss his approaches and solutions. The consultant must indicate acceptance of, and present a serious, workable approach to, the terms of reference. In the discussion of methodology, several questions must be answered to the satisfaction of the client:

*The complete text of Dr. Berger's speech, including Figures 5–2 to 5–7, can be found in *The Function of the Consulting Engineer in the Developing World: Report on the Seminar Held in Teheran, April 1977,* a publication of the International Federation of Consulting Engineers (FIDIC), pp. 104–113.

Only those proposers who have been determined to be **Qualified** in Part I will be rated with respect to the following:

A. EXPERIENCE AND EXPERTISE OF PROPOSER (250 Points)

	Points	Outstanding 10	9	Very Good 8	7	Good 6	5	Adequate 4	3	Marginal 2	1	Inadequate 0	Multiplier	Score
(GENERAL)	General Competence												x 0.75	
	Overseas Experience												x 3.00	
	Home Office Support												x 1.25	
(STUDIES)	Environmental Assessment												x 1.50	
	(As Required) Planning												x 8.75	
	(As Required)												x 1.00	
	Management Staff Organization												x 0.50	
(DESIGN)	(As Required) Design												x 1.00	
	(As Required) Design												x 1.25	
	(As Required) Design												x 2.50	
	(As Required) Design												x 1.25	
	Foundation Investigation												x 0.50	
	Structural Design												x 0.50	
	Electrical Design												x 0.50	
	Construction Supervision												x 0.75	

ITEM A TOTAL

Figure 5–3 Detailed qualification statements for the specific type of project.

B. APPROACH AND WORK PLAN (300 Points)

The proposer's understanding of the problem and the effectiveness of the proposed approach and work plan is evaluated with reference to the criteria below:

Points	OUTSTANDING 10	9	VERY GOOD 8	7	GOOD 6	5	ADEQUATE 4	3	MARGINAL 2	1	INADEQUATE 0	Multiplier	Score
Understanding Problem— Quality of Overview												X 6	
Suitability of Methodology Thoroughness of Work Plan												X 9	
Coverage of All Tasks												X 5	
Division of Effort by Task and Discipline												X 4	
Realistic Manpower Estimate (Excluding final design)												X 6	

ITEM B TOTAL

Figure 5–4 The approach and work plan.

1. Is the general sequence of the work activities shown understandable?
2. Will the schedule of work activities permit incorporation of the scheduled reports?
3. Has the consultant developed necessary data and information required in the terms of reference?
4. Are some activities missing from the terms of reference that should be included?

The consultant should divide the work program into tasks or work activities that are completely delineated so the client can follow the work schedule from beginning to end. Each task should be broken down into divisions of effort or manpower. A detailed division indicates the consultant's familiarity with the project and is therefore a method of determining the manpower required by the task. The consultant should also identify all disciplines required to undertake the project. Disciplines to consider are:

Management
Environment
Civil engineering
Mechanical engineering
Electrical engineering
Foundation and soils
Structural engineering and architecture
Cost specification
Materials requirements
Construction management or supervision

After identifying all disciplines critical to the completion of the project, the client, utilizing the submitted curricula vitae, should ensure that the consultant has proposed competent personnel to manage each discipline. Realistic manpower estimates must be developed to make sure that the job can be accomplished within the specified period of time with the personnel identified through the workplan.

Figure 5–5: One of the most important facets of either the oral interview or submission of technical proposals should be the curricula vitae of the personnel assigned to accomplish the project. The personnel must be experienced in the areas for which they are to be employed. Figure 5–5 demonstrates various rating criteria that should be considered in the grading of personnel to be assigned to the project. After the major items of work have been established from the terms of

PERSONNEL

(450 Points)

Payments:	Qualifying Criteria			Total Points	Task Importance Multiplier	Maximum Score Possible	Score
	Education 0-20	Pertinent Experience 0-50	Developing Nations Experience 0-30				
MANAGEMENT							
1. Administrative					0.15	15	
2. Technical					0.60	60	
PLANNING							
3. Environmentalist					0.35	35	
4. (As Required)					0.15	15	
5. (As Required)					1.85	185	
6. Management Staff Advisor					0.25	25	
(As Required)					(0.25)	(25)	
(As Required)					(0.25)	(25)	
DESIGN							
7. Sanitary/Mechanical Engineer					0.25	25	
8. Civil Engineer					0.15	15	
9. Foundation					0.15	15	
10. Architectural/ Structural					0.15	15	
11. Electrical					0.15	15	
12. Cost/Specification					0.15	15	
SUPPORT							
13. Home Office Technical					0.15	15	

NOTE: Reviewer to attach Computations   **ITEM C TOTAL**

Figure 5-5 Qualifying criteria for personnel.

reference, the consultant should break down his tasks into various divisions and these estimates should be the best method from which the client can grade or rate the proposer through his manpower allocation for individual tasks. (Note: Experience in the project's geographic region and corresponding language ability have significant weight in the Developing Nations Factor.)

KEY STAFF MAN–MONTH ESTIMATE

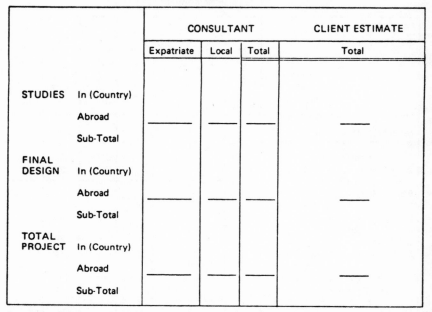

| | | CONSULTANT | | | CLIENT ESTIMATE |
		Expatriate	Local	Total	Total
STUDIES	In (Country)				
	Abroad	___	___	___	___
	Sub-Total				
FINAL DESIGN	In (Country)				
	Abroad	___	___	___	___
	Sub-Total				
TOTAL PROJECT	In (Country)				
	Abroad	___	___	___	___
	Sub-Total				

Figure 5–6 The breakdown of the consultant's key staff estimates.

Figure 5–6: Figure 5–6 shows the breakdown of the consultant's manpower estimates for comparison with the client's estimate.

In summary, the analysis of the consultant's approach—his workplan, personnel, and prior background—truly establishes his suitability. Added to this should be the consultant's general reputation and knowledge of overseas working conditions. These factors provide an excellent evaluation of the consultant's total capability.

Figure 5–7. A recapitulation of the scores of all the various items is shown by Figure 5–7 and the rating scores all totaled. The consultant with the highest rating should be selected to undertake the program.

This method of selection provides reasonable reassurance that the evaluation is based on consistent assessment of the various proposals received and that the proper weight is given to each category of a consultant's qualifications.

Despite efforts to eliminate price as a factor in the evaluation of

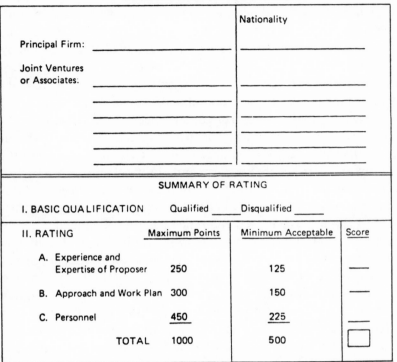

RATING CHART FOR CONSULTANTS

	Nationality
Principal Firm: _____	_____
Joint Ventures or Associates: _____	_____

SUMMARY OF RATING

I. BASIC QUALIFICATION   Qualified _____ Disqualified _____

II. RATING	Maximum Points	Minimum Acceptable	Score
A. Experience and Expertise of Proposer	250	125	—
B. Approach and Work Plan	300	150	—
C. Personnel	450	225	—
TOTAL	1000	500	☐

Figure 5-7 A recapitulation of the various scores.

consultants' qualifications for an assignment, some less knowledgeable clients insist that an estimate of cost be submitted with the proposals. They then assign values to the price figures on a descending scale from the lowest to the highest price quoted. Sometimes, if an estimate is substantially lower than seems reasonable to the client, a low point score is assigned to this factor in the evolution of the proposal. However, there is no way in actual practice to have a disclosed price play a limited role in the selection process; it invariably is weighed heavily, despite the attendant risks to the quality of the project.

Some public clients have been found to be unfamiliar with generally accepted standards used in evaluating engineering firms and their qualifying proposals. On at least two well-known occasions, adverse recommendations were made concerning a firm because of the small size of its brochure and proposal compared with that of another firm. Other qualifications, seemingly unimportant in comparing professional competence of firms, but of significance to foreign clients, are the college degrees, particularly doctorates, held by staff members. A person whose writings have been published is frequently considered superior. The nationality of the firm and its associates may be helpful—or prejudicial. Any operations in Israel almost always preclude one from acceptance in Arab countries.

For private work, an industry or utility such as a power corporation, a railroad, or a water supply company frequently negotiates with only one firm for its requirements, professional or otherwise. The bases for selecting such a firm are the experience record of the firm, personal knowledge of the firm's principals, previous experience with the firm, or a good reference from a colleague.

Exceptions to this procedure arise when an industry already has awarded a prime contract to a general contractor or an equipment manufacturer for a package or turnkey job. All too often the prime contractor will follow the practice he is accustomed to and request bids for design of the plant or ancillary facilities required when his own technical staff is not adequate for the work. A similar situation may arise when a general contractor or a manufacturer puts in his bid for the prime contract for a turnkey job and asks an engineer to submit a price for his part of the work. This introduces a point of professional ethics as to whether, in complying, the consultant is participating in a price competition which is, of course, contrary to professional standards.

Contractual Arrangements

After the evaluation of proposals has been completed, the client invites the selected firm for negotiations. Typically, a negotiation starts with a discussion of "terms of reference," the comments made by the consultants on the scope of services, and the consultant's proposed work program. Then staffing is discussed and agreed upon.

This is followed by discussion of budgets. The consultants are requested to submit a breakdown of the proposed "agreed fixed rates" for each man on the team. The elements of these rates include the basic salary of the staff, the social benefits payable by the firm (i.e. social insurance, vacations, sick leave, etc.), the firm's overhead, and the firm's fee (profit). For extended periods of time abroad, a component for overseas allowance may also be included (usually as a supplement to basic salary). In addition, agreement is reached on foreign currency expenditures, which include a subsistence allowance (per diem) and reimbursement for some of the other incidental expenditures to be made by the consultants in the country of the study.

Needless to say, contract negotiations should be handled only by experienced staff of the consultant, preferably two or three persons, and reviewed by the comptroller of the firm and one or more of the firm's principals. Valuable contributions can be made to the contract terms by local attorneys familiar with local laws as well as the legal system on which those laws were based; in foreign countries, for example, English Common Law or the Napoleonic Code. Approvals of the contract by the proper local officials authorized to enter into contracts is essential. These should include not only the head of the agency, but also its counsel and particularly the government's financial officer.

Chapter

ECONOMICS OF CONSULTING ENGINEERING

Richard H. Stanley
President, Stanley Consultants, Inc.

"Is it a business or a profession?" This is a classic question about consulting engineering practice. The classic answer is that it is both. But this begs the question of how a consulting engineering practice can meet sometimes conflicting business and professional demands.

Because it is a profession, the practice of consulting engineering must hold to high standards of service to its clients and the general public. Professional registration laws place a heavy burden on those who practice, requiring that they certify that their work is consistent with the public health, safety, and welfare. Consulting engineers deal in professional services, applying the time and talent of their professional, technical, and support staff members to solving client problems and meeting client and public needs. Such personal and professional services cannot be neatly defined and specified. Not infrequently, the professional discipline of a consulting engineer requires "second mile" effort in the client and public interest, even though the economic burden of this effort falls heavily upon the firm. The firm will soon lose any semblance of professional reputation if it short-cuts service to the client because the budget for the engagement has been expended or if it fails to consider the public impact of the work even though the fee is not sufficient.

Conversely, a consulting engineering firm will not be viable if it neglects sound business practices. It must negotiate and collect fees for its services which cover all costs of doing business and provide a fair return on the capital invested. Only a profitable practice can remain in business long and, therefore, be in a position to practice professionally. But excessive emphasis on financial results will inevitably chill the firm's commitment to professional excellence and service to clients and the public.

The need for a firm to chart a course that satisfies both business and professional responsibilities is clear. The method is not. While statements of principle and objective are important (and every consulting engineering firm should have them), the real working out of professional and business responsibilities is done in the day-to-day actions and decisions of the principals and staff members. Hence, a key to achieving a successful balance between business and professional demands lies in having the ownership control and management of the firm in the hands of design professionals who are sensitive to sound business practices. Consulting engineering firms have failed because their engineer principals were not sufficiently committed to sound business practices. Others have failed because their nonengineer owners and managers placed too much emphasis on financial results and neglected professional responsibilities. It is for this reason that American Consulting Engineers Council (ACEC) has consistently emphasized the importance of independent professional ownership and control.

Economic Viability

What, then, are the elements of economic viability that permit a firm to succeed economically while it also succeeds professionally?

At the outset, it must be recognized that successful consulting engineering practice is built upon the human resource capabilities of the firm. The quality and scope of services that can be offered are limited by the commitment and capabilities of the staff members that the firm attracts, develops, and retains. As discussed in Chapter 4, this means that the consulting engineering firm must pay close attention to personnel administration practices, technical and professional development of staff members, and their career development. Typically, two-thirds of the revenue is spent for staff salaries and payroll-related costs. The human resources of a firm are its greatest asset, and this asset merits careful nurturing and development.

Good economic management does not just happen. Economic viability is built on a well-designed system of financial and managerial accounting. Such a system, developed specifically to meet the firm's circumstances and needs, provides the economic data that are the basis for good management.

With proper emphasis on human resources and a fully adequate accounting system, the principals and managers can focus their attention on key decision areas that affect economic viability. These include the following items which are discussed in greater depth in later sections of this chapter.

- A satisfactory balance between workload and staff
- Competent planning and control of each client engagement
- Negotiation of a satisfactory professional-services contract and an adequate fee for the services provided on each engagement
- Good management of the firm's cash flow
- Adequate financing of the firm's operations
- Risk management

Fundamentals

Managers and future managers need a good understanding of basic accounting and financial matters. A course or two in accounting is highly recommended. Thorough knowledge of the financial system and management reports used by the firm is essential. The following brief overview of accounting reports for consulting engineering firms will provide perspective on the economics of practice.

Accounting Reports

The two major purposes of an accounting system are financial accounting and managerial accounting. Accounting reports can be regular (prepared at regularly stated intervals for specific persons), or special (prepared intermittently in response to a manager's request).

Financial accounting provides information primarily for the historical record and for the use of parties outside the business or not directly involved in managing the business. This may include shareholders or partners (in their role as owners), creditors, government agencies, etc. Financial accounting is externally oriented and it usually generates historical reports summarizing the financial history and position of a firm as a whole.

In contrast, managerial accounting is concerned with accounting information that is useful to managers within the firm: cost, revenue, or profit associated with a particular engagement or with some portion of the firm's total operation. Managerial accounting reports are tailored to the specific management systems and accountabilities within the firm. Their purpose is to provide a basis for managing current and future work.

Each consulting engineering firm must establish systems and assign responsibilities for the generation of financial and managerial accounting reports. The systems and assignments also should provide checks against possible misappropriation of company assets and provide suitable audit records and procedures.

The organization of the firm for financial management varies greatly with the size of firm. However, financial management must include sufficient attention to areas such as accounting, auditing, budgeting, cash management, capital expenditures, financial statements, government regulation, insurance, inventories, payrolls, purchasing, statistical analysis, and taxes. Some firms assign an engineering principal to supervise financial management. Others staff this responsibility with professionally trained accountants or business managers reporting to the managing principals.

Many firms use an accrual basis for accounting reports. Such firms estimate revenues earned on partially completed engagements, usually on a percent-of-completion basis, and also measure expenses incurred even though the expense is incurred in advance of cash expenditure. This system provides the best basis for managerial reports. Other firms use a cash-basis accounting system that records only cash receipts and cash disbursements.

Financial Characteristics

Accounting and financial management procedures for a firm offering professional services differ in degree but are similar to those used by manufacturing organizations. Some significant differences merit mention.

A professional services firm does not have physical inventories; services cannot be stored. Hence, fluctuations in volume create unique staffing, cost and revenue problems. However, consulting engineering firms do have work in process in the form of partially completed engagements.

A professional services firm is labor-intensive, or human resources-intensive. Relatively little capital is required. The staff members of firms are the most important resource. This makes a professional services firm more difficult to control and more attention must be devoted to day-to-day performance. It is difficult, however, to measure and control the quantity of services rendered. The quality of services can seldom be inspected in advance.

Professional services firms are usually small. Thus, top managers have tended to use personal observations in controlling and motivating managers and other staff members. For this reason, accounting systems in professional service organizations tend to be less advanced than those found in manufacturing firms. However, recognition of the importance of more sophisticated financial and managerial systems is growing and will continue to do so in the future.

Financial Accounting Reports

The end results of financial accounting are four basic financial statements: the balance sheet, which reports the financial position of the firm at one moment in time, usually the end of a month, quarter, or year; the income (or operating) statement, which summarizes the financial performance of the firm over a period of time, usually a month, quarter, or year; the statement of owners' (partners', stockholders', etc.) equity, which summarizes changes in the equity position of the owners over a period of time, usually a year; and the statement of changes in financial position, which summarizes changes in working capital over a period of time, usually a year. The first two are in general use and are discussed below.

Balance Sheet

The balance sheet reports the assets, liabilities, and equities of a firm at one point in time. Assets are listed on the left, liabilities and equities on the right. Figure 6–1 shows a basic classification of balance sheet accounts.

An asset is an item owned or leased by a company which has a value that can be measured objectively in monetary terms. Assets may be tangible, like a building, or intangible, like goodwill. They represent property or property rights. Major asset accounts include:

1. *Accounts receivable:* an amount that is owed to a firm, usually by one of its clients, as a result of a billing for services.
2. *Work in process:* the revenue value of work performed on jobs which is in excess of the amount billed to clients.
3. *Prepaid expenses:* services and certain intangibles purchased prior to the period during which their benefits are received. They are treated as assets until consumed.
4. *Total current assets:* the total of the above items which are assets that either are in the form of cash or are expected to be converted into cash within one year.
5. *Land, building, and equipment:* physical assets used and either owned or leased by the firm. Such assets usually are shown at the price at which they were acquired. Accounting practice now requires that long-term leases be capitalized.
6. *Accumulated depreciation:* an account showing the total amount of depreciation of an asset that has been accumulated to date. Depreciation is the method for recognizing a portion of the cost of a fixed asset as an expense throughout each year of its estimated life. Several methods can be used.
7. *Total fixed assets:* the net value of tangible properties of relatively long life that are generally used to produce goods or services.
8. *Goodwill:* an intangible asset paid for by the firm to acquire a favorable location or reputation. Other examples are trademarks and patents.

Liabilities represent claims against assets that are held by creditors. They include:

1. *Accounts payable:* an amount owed to a creditor, usually due upon receipt of billing.

Balance Sheet
(In Thousands of Dollars)

ASSETS	DECEMBER 31	
	19X1	19X2
Current assets:		
Cash	20	30
Accounts receivable	50	60
Work in process	60	40
Prepaid expenses	10	10
Total current assets	140	140
Fixed assets:		
Land	30	30
Buildings and equipment	130	150
Less accumulated depreciation	60	70
Net buildings and equipment	70	80
Total fixed assets	100	110
Other assets:		
Goodwill and patents	10	10
Total assets	250	260

LIABILITIES AND EQUITY	DECEMBER 31	
	19X1	19X2
Current liabilities:		
Accounts payable	25	20
Accrued wages and taxes	35	30
Estimated income taxes payable	10	15
Total current liabilities	70	65
Long-term liabilities:		
Mortgage note, 12 percent	50	35
Stockholders' equity:		
Common stock (500 shares outstanding)	80	80
Retained earnings	50	80
Total capital	130	160
Total liabilities and equity	250	260

Figure 6–1 Basic classification of balance sheet accounts. (Note that numbers are not typical.)

2. *Accrued wages:* a liability arising because an expense occurs in a period prior to the related payment.
3. *Total current liabilities:* obligations that become due within a short period (no longer than a year). They represent claims against all assets of the firm.
4. *Long-term liabilities:* the claim of a creditor, usually long-term in duration.

Owners' equity is the net worth or value of the business. Net worth is equal to assets less liabilities. In an incorporated firm, the owners' equity or net worth is expressed in stock accounts and retained earnings. In an unincorporated firm, the owners' equity will be expressed in accounts such as partners' equity or proprietors' equity.

It is important to note that this report is called a balance sheet because assets are equal to liabilities plus net worth. The left side of the sheet balances the right.

Income Statement

The income, or operating, statement is a statement of revenues and expenses for a given period (month, quarter, year). It reflects the results of the firm's operations (transactions) that produce a financial gain or loss for the period. An increase in equity is called revenue. A decrease in equity is called an expense. This, in turn, shows the extent to which equity has increased or decreased during the accounting period. Figure 6-2 shows an example of a basic operating statement account classification.

Major operating statement accounts include:

1. *Revenue:* an increase in owners' equity resulting from operations. For a consulting engineering firm this is the recorded recognition of income for professional services performed for clients.
2. *Direct costs:* the costs directly expended to perform services for a client. They include cost of time of staff members working on the engagements and expenses. Direct time (sometimes called direct labor) charges usually are extended from time charges recorded on time-charge forms turned in by each staff member. Some firms extend direct time costs at base salary rates. Others use rates that include both salary and salary-related costs. Direct expenses are items of expense which are directly applicable to

Operating Statement 19XX
(In Thousands of Dollars)

		DOLLARS
Gross revenues		750
Direct costs:		
Time	300	
Expenses	50	
Less: Total direct costs		350
Gross margin		400
Indirect Costs:		
Time	185	
Expenses	180	
Less: Total indirect costs		365
Operating margin from consulting		35
Other income		5
Income before taxes		40
Taxes		10
Net income		30

Figure 6–2 Basic classification of operating statement accounts. (Note that numbers are not typical.)

the client engagement such as travel, out-of-pocket expenses, telephone and telegraph, materials, supplies, printing, and similar expenses. They also may include charges for computer services and services obtained from outside the firm. Total direct costs are the sum of direct time and expense.

3. *Gross margin:* the excess of revenue dollars over direct costs.
4. *Indirect costs:* both time and expense which are not directly applicable to a specific job number. Table 6-1 shows a listing of typical indirect cost items.
5. *Margin from consulting services:* the gain or loss resulting from subtracting all direct and indirect costs from revenues.
6. *Other income:* any other sources of income not related directly to the practice of consulting engineering.
7. *Income before taxes:* the sum of margin from consulting services and other income.

8. *Taxes:* federal, state, and perhaps local taxes on income.
9. *Net income:* income after deduction of taxes.

The last two items appear only on corporate operating statements. They are not applicable to partnerships or sole proprietorships.

Typical Financial Ratios

The financial ratios typical for consulting engineering firms vary widely. This is because firms differ greatly in size, capitalization, and philosophy of financial management. Nevertheless, Table 6-2 will serve to give a general indication of typical financial ratios.

TABLE 6-1
Basic Classification of Indirect Cost Accounts

Administration
Business development
Technical development
Professional development
Recruiting
Staff member relations
Supplies, equipment, and maintenance
Office operation
   Rent
   Depreciation
   Utilities
Business licenses and memberships
Auditing services
Legal services
Dues and charitable contributions
Staff member benefits
   Payroll taxes
   Vacations, holidays, and sick leave
   Group benefit programs
Taxes
   Property
   Sales and use
   Income

TABLE 6-2

Typical Financial Ratios—Consulting Engineering Firms

RATIO	TYPICAL	TYPICAL RANGE
Revenue to assets		
(Turnover on assets)	2.5	2.0–4.0
Revenue to net worth		
(Turnover on net worth)	5.0	3.0–10.0
Revenue per employee		
(1979—includes all employees)	$33,000	$25,000–$45,000
Total current assets to revenue	0.25	0.15–0.45
Total current liabilities to revenue	0.12	0.05–0.20
Current ratio (current assets to		
current liabilities)	2.0	1.3–3.5
Overhead ratio (indirect costs as a		
percentage of direct salaries)	150%	125–175%

Managerial Accounting Reports

Because managerial accounting reports provide information useful to managers, they tend to be custom-tailored to the specific needs, organization, and assignments of responsibility within the firm. However, the firm does not have total freedom. Managerial accounting reports must have an auditable relationship to the financial accounting reports. The sum of the parts of the operation reflected in managerial accounting reports must equal the whole of the financial operation reflected in the financial accounting reports. Further, some managerial accounting reports are used to support client billings and fee negotiations. For this reason, they must be consistent with generally accepted accounting practices and any specific accounting requirements of the client. In developing its system of managerial accounting reports, each consulting firm must carefully consider both its own managerial requirements and those of its clientele. Because of the pervasiveness of federal funding and regulation, federal cost and accounting principles have become a very significant factor in design of managerial accounting reports.

For these reasons, it is difficult to generalize on the managerial accounting reports of consulting engineering firms. However, the basic managerial needs, and the types of information required to fill these needs, can be described.

Cost-Accounting System

The foundation of managerial accounting reports is the firm's cost-accounting system. As noted earlier, the operating statement reports general cost categories such as direct time, direct expenses, indirect time, and indirect expenses. Theoretically, a firm could operate with only these four "pockets" for the collection of costs. This might be sufficient if the firm had only one client and one or two people. However, consulting engineering firms serve many clients on a wide variety of engagements. They may have many staff members whose assignments and functions differ greatly.

This mandates a cost-accounting system that provides a much more detailed classification of costs than that provided by those shown on the operating statement. To do otherwise would forfeit any opportunity for managerial control. The degree of detail necessarily varies from firm to firm. However, each firm should have a system which is flexible enough to permit development and refinement as the firm's needs change and which is not more detailed than required for the firm's present needs. Judgment is involved.

As a minimum, the cost-accounting system should provide for separation of direct time and expense costs into separate accounts for each client engagement. This permits budgeting costs for the engagement, controlling costs to budget, and recording costs for client billing. The cost-accounting system of nearly all firms carries the direct-job costs to much greater detail. In most instances, it is desirable to have a system that permits separating the costs charged to each engagement into various phases of the work. Each phase may be further subdivided by the professional or technical discipline involved. There also may be subdivisions that reflect departmental or other organizational unit responsibility for the work and associated budget. Such cost subdivisions may result in a classification of accounts which provides a system of 5 to 10 or more digits. All direct costs, whether time or expense, are then coded so that they can be distributed properly to the various accounts.

The indirect cost picture is similar. The primary exception is that costs are defined as "indirect" because they are not directly allocable to a specific client engagement. Therefore, the cost-accounting system for indirect costs generally provides for division of indirect costs into various functional categories. These may include categories such as those shown in Table 6–1. Generally, there is further subdivision of many of these accounts by department or other organizational unit responsible for budget control. Usually, separate account numbers are used for time and expense for the same function because the control methods for time and expense differ.

The degree of refinement of the cost-accounting system tends to increase with size of firm and complexity of its engagements and operations. In developing its cost-accounting system, each firm must make a reasoned judgment as to what is an optimal system for its circumstances. A system that is too simple will not provide an adequate basis for managerial reporting and control. A system that is too complex adds cost and increases the chances of bad input data. The law of diminishing returns applies to increasing job cost-accounting system detail.

Whatever system is established, it must be well understood and rigorously followed by all within the consulting engineering firm. Those who are or would be managers must have an understanding of the system second only to that of the accounting and financial people who operate it. Both financial and managerial accounting reports are based on the data gathered by the firm's cost-accounting system. The value of these reports depends on the accuracy of the data input and the understanding of the basis on which they are generated.

The following discussion outlines several basic managerial accounting reports which, in one form or another, are generally necessary for effective management of consulting engineering practice.

Direct Cost Reports for Each Engagement

Those responsible for managing the work on a client engagement need regular reporting on the financial status of the engagement. This report should include the following basic information for the engagement and each major portion of it: fee, budget, costs to date, costs required to complete, revenue earned, and billings to date. In addition, it is generally helpful to include various percentages or ratios on this report, covering items such as percent complete, gross margin (revenue less direct cost), ratio of gross margin to direct time, percent budget used, and other factors deemed helpful to the managers of the engagement.

If the firm is sizable enough to have departmental or other organizational responsibility for various phases or other portions of the work, there should be reports to each accountable manager covering costs, budget, ratios, etc., on the part of the work for which that manager is accountable.

Nearly all firms generate reports for engagements on a cumulative to-date basis. Many firms refine these reports by adding the financial changes during an appropriate fiscal period (month, quarter, half, or year). This approach gives a more accurate picture of current rather than past results and thus facilitates current management of the engagement. These reports, like other managerial reports, must be made available to the accountable managers on a timely and frequent basis so that the information can be the basis for management decision and action.

Scheduled Workload

Another necessary management accounting report is a periodic schedule of workload. This report should show the hours scheduled to be worked on each client engagement over a reasonable time period, preferably at least six months into the future. Depending on size of firm, the scheduled hours may be subdivided by phases, discipline, departmental or organizational responsibility, and even individual assignment. Schedules should be shown month by month or week by week. The report should also show, for comparison purposes, the staff members assigned to or available to be assigned to the various engagements, phases, disciplines, etc.

The hours scheduled on this document should reflect the best judgment of hours required in the various fiscal periods to meet engagement requirements. The report generally shows budgeted hours and hours used to date as well. Note that hours scheduled for completion may be greater or less than the hours budgeted less hours used to date. The objective of this report is to have a good understanding of the workload ahead, whether or not it is consistent with budgets for the various engagements.

With proper summaries and totals, this report provides managers of each engagement with information on whether the engagement is properly staffed and moving along on budget. More global summaries show the overall loading picture for departments and the firm as a whole. This is essential to decisions regarding staff assignments, recruiting, work schedules, ability to commit on schedules for new engagements, and similar matters.

Time Utilization Report

This report shows the charging of staff time—to direct work, to overhead accounts, or to personal time (vacation, sick leave, etc.). At any given time, a consulting engineering firm has a comparatively fixed staff complement. The total time of all staff members must be charged to one account or another. Experience demonstrates that the profitability of a firm is very sensitive to the percentage of total time of staff members being used on client engagements and, hence, charged to direct time accounts. An increase in this percentage indicates both an increase in the amount of time that can produce revenue from clients and a decrease in indirect costs.

The report is developed directly from the time-charge forms prepared by all members of the firm. The report, if timely, can give a good current indication of how staff time is being utilized and provide a basis for management decisions on staff levels and assignments. This report is generally most beneficial to departmental and higher managers.

Indirect Cost Reports

Indirect cost reports show the indirect time and expense incurred during a given fiscal period (month, quarter, half, or year). In addition, they should show the budgets established for the period as well as the percent of budget used. With proper summaries and totals, indirect cost reports should place information in the hands of responsible managers so that they can make decisions regarding indirect cost management. Costs can also be compared against progress on programs such as business development, technical development, recruiting, etc.

New Business Results

A report showing new business results for a given fiscal period is another essential managerial report. At a minimum, it shows the new engagements contracted and changes in scope and fee on previously contracted work. In larger firms, new business reports may be summarized by type of client, location, type of work, and perhaps other factors germane to the firm's planning and management. New business reports may also summarize the new business prospects which are known and being developed.

These reports provide managers responsible for business development with a good indication of the results of their efforts and a general picture of prospective engagements.

Accounts Receivable

For each client engagement, and perhaps various phases of the engagement, this report should show the total amount of billings submitted to the client but not yet paid. In addition, it should show an aged analysis of these amounts, i.e., how long they have been outstanding. It may also be desirable to include information on revenue earned and total billings to date on each engagement.

This information provides the managers of each engagement with data for client follow-up regarding payment of billings. It provides general and financial managers with good information on trends and problem areas in client credit. Such reports can also be summarized to show payment patterns for various categories of clients.

Cash-Flow Projection

Both short- and long-term cash-flow projections are helpful for managing fiscal requirements.

The short-term cash-flow projection should show current bank balances, receipts, and expenditures during the last fiscal period (week or month) and projected cash receipts and expenditures during the next two or more fiscal periods. Such information is necessary for short-term cash planning. The projection may indicate need for short-term borrowing, possibility of short-term investment, need to defer expenditures or accelerate receipts, etc. It is primarily of benefit to the financial officer of the firm.

The longer-term cash-flow projection shows estimated changes in the cash position over the next 12 to 24 months or longer. This projection resembles a *pro forma* statement of changes in financial position and is normally prepared by the financial officer of the firm. It is of great assistance to the general managers in planning financing, including arranging for lines of credit, sale of additional equity, declaration of dividends, ability to handle proposed investments using current earnings, and many similar financial planning issues.

Other Managerial Accounting Reports

The possibility of other managerial accounting reports is endless. The objective of any managerial report is to provide information for action and decision making to appropriate managers. Thus, the managerial needs will dictate the reports required.

It is proper, however, to caution that both regular and special managerial reports should be scrutinized regularly to be sure that their value as a decision-making tool justifies the cost of preparation. Needs and circumstances change, but accounting reports, once established, often are continued without regard to justification. On the other hand, capricious change in report content and format should be avoided. When changes are made, there is a risk that historic data series will be broken or lost.

Automated or Manual Accounting

With rapidly decreasing costs of computer capability, only the smallest consulting engineering firms should rely on manual accounting systems. Even very small firms may benefit from a computer-based system using a computer service center. Larger firms are moving rapidly toward the use of on-line terminals to provide ready accounting information and reduce the amount of hard copy distributed. Computer terminals will never totally replace hard copy because periodic reports are needed for records and reference. Nonetheless, the most effective accounting systems of the future will use on-line data terminals for a great deal of managerial accounting information. Hard copy reports will be limited to general trends and information, and the more detailed data will be available for call-up and analysis when the general reports indicate problem areas and need for action and decision.

Balancing Workload and Staff

Maintaining a tolerable balance between workload and staff is one of the most difficult aspects of managing a consulting engineering practice.

The way in which a firm manages this balance is fundamental to its economic success. If a firm commits to client demands without attention to staff availability and capability, it will experience rapid increases and decreases in staff and periods of heavy overload and underload. This imposes both risks and costs. In the first place, it is very expensive to operate with widely fluctuating staff levels. The costs of recruiting and terminating staff members are high and require substantial amounts of principals' time. Less obvious, but perhaps even more costly, is the fact that new staff members who are unfamiliar with the firm's operating procedures and standards are less likely to work efficiently and more likely to be the source of misunderstandings or errors. Average staff tenure is likely to be low, eroding the firm's ability to foster career development of staff members. In the long run, this may make it difficult for the firm to retain and develop competent managers and future principals. In addition, it is hazardous for a firm to commit itself to a client schedule which requires unrealistic recruitment of additional staff. A firm which fails to deliver on schedule injures its reputation and credibility.

At the other extreme, a consulting engineering firm can operate with too much emphasis on its own convenience. It might operate with staff levels normally higher than its usual workload. This will cause high overheads because much of the staff time will frequently not be chargeable to client engagements. Alternatively, the firm could operate with a fairly limited staff and take only those engagements which fit or could be made to fit within staff capability. Clients are unlikely to be pleased with either the prospect of paying very high fees to support a high overhead or the prospect of changing their schedules to fit the convenience of the firm. Thus, unless the consulting engineering firm has such a unique capability that clients are willing to engage it on its own terms, an inflexible approach undoubtedly will prove disastrous.

What procedure, then, should be used to manage the workload and staff balance?

Know Where You Are

The first step is to know what the balance is at any given time. This requires a regularly scheduled workload report as previously discussed. The loading picture can change quickly, sometimes for reasons that are within the consulting engineering firm's control and sometimes for reasons that are not. New engagements may be added to the loading. Existing engagements may be canceled or delayed. Staff availability may change due to new staff additions, illnesses, vacations, or terminations. Progress on the work may be faster or slower than anticipated, leading to changes in estimated hours required to complete the various work elements.

A current workload report forms the basis for decisions that will determine whether the firm is able to maintain a reasonable workload and staff balance.

Develop Staff Flexibility

The discipline capabilities and specialties of consulting engineering firm staff members are developed and selected on the basis of the firm's normal engagements and load. The level of expertise and the degree of staff specialization are dictated by the firm's practice and clientele.

However, staff flexibility will greatly increase the firm's ability to cope with varying loads. An example is civil engineers who can competently handle moderately complex work in a variety of areas such as structures, hydraulics, and transportation facilities. When the firm has a heavy workload of one particular type, such engineers can shift from one kind of work to another. While specialists undoubtedly bring greater competence to their subdiscipline, they may be less able to handle other work. For this reason, most firms tend to have comparatively few specialists and a larger number of more flexible generalists. The optimum mix of disciplines, specialists, and generalists is elusive, and must be carefully selected and nurtured within the firm.

Manage Job Schedules

Careful management of job schedules will help to balance workload and staff. Some elements of any engagement schedule are on the critical path; others are not. Careful study of project schedules may suggest areas where work elements can be accelerated or delayed to fit staff availability.

Another element is managing schedule commitments on new engagements. The consequences of an unrealistic promise to meet a given client schedule are likely to be more severe than the consequences of being realistic about the schedule at the outset. While some clients may decide to go elsewhere for a particular engagement if the consulting engineering firm is unable to meet their schedule, they are far more likely never to return to a firm that fails to deliver on a schedule commitment. Avoiding commitment to schedules which cannot be met is the best practice. Many clients have more flexibility in their schedule than they initially indicate, and they may be willing to adapt to reasonable adjustments. Even the client who cannot accept schedule changes and goes elsewhere will have a higher opinion of the firm for its realism and honesty. It is better to lose an engagement by being realistic on schedule commitments than to lose a client through lack of realism.

Develop the Ability to Change Staff Size

Within reasonable limits, the consulting engineering firm needs the ability to adjust its size of staff. Several approaches can be used. Overtime will, for short periods, increase staff capability almost in proportion to the additional hours worked. However, evidence indicates that the extra production diminishes after several weeks.

Staff levels can be increased by additional recruiting. The costs of recruiting additional staff members may range from 5 to 40 percent or more of the annual salary of the new person. Costs of recruiting tend to increase with the professional and experience level of the position as well as with the relocation distance involved and the comparative scarcity of the particular discipline. The time required to fill a position varies similarly. Many weeks or months may be required to fill critical positions. New staff members require orientation and are not likely to be able to carry major leadership responsibility for some time. For these reasons, recruiting from outside the organization should be considered primarily a means of adding to permanent staff, rather than a means of dealing with short-term workload and staff balance.

Another approach is contract staff from another firm. Firms in the contract employee business may have staff members available who can be added temporarily. The cost of such contract staff members is invariably higher than the appropriate salary for the position because the contracting firm must cover its overhead and profit. Nonetheless, competent staff can sometimes be used to meet short-term demands. Because such staff members are not permanent, they should be used to provide capacity rather than leadership for the work.

Some firms also have developed a cadre of on-call staff which may include retired members of the firm or others who are known to have the capabilities needed and who are available to help with heavy workloads.

Planning and Controlling Each Engagement

The financial performance of a consulting engineering firm is a function of the aggregate financial performance on each client engagement. Therefore, individual engagements must be planned and controlled to produce good results.

Planning the Engagement

Planning includes deciding what will be done, who will do it, when it will be done, and how it will be done. Before any significant amount of work is undertaken on the engagement, a complete plan for the effort should be developed.

Unlike the specification for the purchase of a product, there can never be a precise and adequate definition of a professional service.

One simply cannot define matters like degree of care, imagination, creativity, and professional judgment in precise terms. For this reason, the best approach to planning an engagement is to have the planning done by competent professionals in the fields involved in the client and consulting engineering organizations. While the written plan and scope of services developed by these professionals will still fall short of precision, the mutual professional trust and understanding developed in the process of planning and contract-scope development provides the best probability of a good plan and a good result from that plan.

The division of planning effort between the client and the consulting engineer varies. Clients with significant in-house professional design capability often work very closely with the consulting engineering firm as the scope and plan for the engagement are developed. This is usually the most constructive approach. Clients who do not have in-house professional design capability often rely heavily on the consulting engineer to develop a proposed scope and plan. In such instances, the client should, before giving approval, review the recommendations of the consulting engineer to be sure that they meet client needs. Some clients with extensive in-house professional design capability develop scope and plan independently, without involving the consulting engineer. Such clients often forgo the opportunity to take advantage of the consulting engineer's special capabilities and ideas on alternative approaches.

Planning is usually accomplished in stages. Precontract planning includes those steps necessary to conclude negotiations between the client and the consulting engineer on the contract for professional services. The client's role is the strongest in precontract planning. Postcontract planning includes review of precontract plans for changed conditions resulting from contract negotiations. It then moves to a more detailed planning of the effort. Normally, the consulting engineer has the primary role in postcontract planning. Sometimes the work required to define and plan an engagement is more extensive than the consulting engineer can reasonably afford to undertake without compensation. In such cases it may be appropriate for the client and the consulting engineer to enter into a contract for the development of a detailed plan and approach for carrying out the subsequent larger effort. This scope might also include analysis of feasibility, recommendation of financing, and other related matters.

Regardless of the method used, the division of effort between the client and consulting engineer, and the planning schedule, the objective of planning the engagement is to develop a detailed description of what should take place on the engagement. This should include the following:

1. A detailed description of the scope of the effort, including the results or objectives to be achieved.
2. Identification of interfaces and linkages between work to be done by the consulting engineer, by the client, and by others.
3. Description of the various work elements required to achieve the stated objective.
4. A budget for the time and expense required to complete each work element.
5. A schedule for the engagement and its work elements.
6. Assignments of the persons who will work on the project team, from both the consulting engineer and the client organizations. This includes descriptions of responsibility and authority.
7. A detailed plan for communications, including reviews and approvals.

Such a plan, developed by design professionals on the basis of mutual confidence, provides the best possible basis for a successful engagement. The plan for the engagement is not immutable. Circumstances often change during an engagement. But a well-documented plan is the best basis for determining when a change is necessary. Plan changes are developed following the same procedures used for the initial planning.

Controlling the Engagement

Controlling is a management function that includes directing, monitoring, and acting to be sure that the plan is carried out and that the objectives are met.

Controlling requires good communication to make sure that all who are working on the engagement are aware of the plan and that this understanding persists throughout the engagement. Budgets, schedules, and work outputs should be monitored closely to identify actual or potential deviations from plan. Managerial accounting reports provide a significant amount of data which can be used for this purpose. Prompt corrective action should be taken when needed.

Effective controlling also requires motivating and supervising people assigned to the engagement and giving attention to their performance and development.

Quality control is also important. Each firm should have well-defined quality-control policies and procedures. Work on engagements should not be considered satisfactory unless it has been performed in a manner consistent with these procedures. Further, because consulting engineering services are professional in nature, total reliance cannot be placed on policies and procedures. The actual output of major work elements must be subjected to the judgment and review of professionals other than those doing the work to be sure that the work meets the firm's professional standards.

While control procedures will vary with circumstances, an indispensable ingredient is that of paying attention. Many control problems can be traced to incomplete communication, making assumptions rather than learning the facts, and a lack of follow-through. Thoroughness, watchfulness, and attention to the overall results are essential.

With a good plan for the engagement and effective control of the work in accordance with the plan, the results should be satisfactory from both a business and a professional viewpoint.

Professional Services Contracts and Fees

Consulting engineering firms offer professional services to clients for a fee. Substantially, the clients are purchasing the time and talent of a firm's staff members.

While there may have been a time when formal, written, professional services contracts and detailed fee negotiations were not necessary, a time when both consulting engineers and clients would rely on a handshake and good faith, that time has long since passed. In today's turbulent, litigious society, it is of great importance that the understandings and agreements between the client and the consulting engineer be reduced to writing.

Contract Documents

The purpose of a professional services contract is to set forth the total understandings on the services to be performed. The contract should deal specifically with the following areas: the description of the services to be provided by the consulting engineer, probably including a description of services which may be excluded from the consulting engineer's work; a description of services to be provided by the owner; a description of services to be provided by others, if applicable; the fee or compensation to be paid to the consulting engineer, including payment procedures and terms; a schedule for execution of the services; procedures for changing scope of services; procedures for termination of the contract; and such other special provisions as may be appropriate. In many respects, the professional services contract reduces to writing the precontract planning for the engagement. It documents the mutual responsibilities between the client and the consulting engineer.

Several points must be kept in mind when preparing professional services contracts. First, the contract should be sufficiently complete and explicit to permit the two parties to deal with problems and disagreements if they should occur. While both client and consulting engineer want productive and harmonious relationships throughout the engagement, the written contract provides the means to handle disputes if they occur. Second, the language of the professional services contract should deal with responsibilities to third parties. Increasingly, parties other than those who signed the contract may be involved in disputes or litigation related to the contract. Third, the language in the professional services contract should be consistent with language in other contract documents, such as those for the construction work related to the engagement. Inconsistencies between contract documents related to the same engagement can create difficult and costly litigation hazards.

Perhaps the best work being done today on engineer-, owner-, and construction-related documents is that of the Engineers' Joint Contract Documents Committee, which includes participation by the Professional Engineers in Private Practice (a practice division of the National Society of Professional Engineers), ACEC, and the American Society of Civil Engineers. This committee publishes and updates a complete series of contract and other construction-related documents. They are based on the extensive practical experience of the representatives of the three participating associations. Experienced legal counsel provides guidance based on both historic and recent litigation and other problems. Construction contract law is rather specialized. Most practicing attorneys have comparatively little experience in this area and the availability of committee documents is a great service to all parties concerned. Copies of these documents can be purchased from any one of the three participating organizations.

Another organization that has done extensive work in construction-related contracts and other documents is the American Institute of Architects. These documents tend to be focused more on building projects than on heavier engineering construction. In addition, the Construction Specifications Institute, Inc., the Associated General Contractors of America, and others have developed useful documents.

Consulting engineers should obtain legal counsel regarding development, use, or modification of contracts and other construction-related documents. Each firm should develop and maintain an ongoing working relationship with competent legal counsel experienced in construction law documents and practices. Many consulting engineering firms develop internal paralegal capability and some have in-house legal counsel. However, such internal capability is seldom, if ever, a total replacement for external expertise.

The existence and use of well-drawn contracts is vital to the economic viability of consulting engineering practice. The absence of such documents and flaws or omissions in their content can be both costly and disconcerting.

Fees for Services

Consulting engineering services are custom-tailored to the specific needs of the client and the engagement. The fees result from the precontract planning of the engagement. In general, the fee charged must cover the direct time costs of those who will be working on the engagement; the direct expenses to be incurred in carrying out the engagement (including any subcontracts for services from others); appropriate overheads, including indirect time and expense, which are allocable to the direct time and are usually expressed as a percentage of direct time cost; and an additional margin that compensates the consulting engineer for the risks, income taxes, return on assets employed, and profit.

The best method of developing a rigorous fee estimate is to take the precontract plan for the work and estimate the direct time and expense costs that will be required to perform each work element. Appropriate indirect costs and margin are added. Fee estimates should be prepared in a manner consistent with the cost-accounting system of the firm. The cost-accounting system should provide historical cost information which will be useful in fee estimating. Also, estimates consistent with the system facilitate job budgeting and control once the fee is negotiated. Finally, the cost-accounting system provides the basis for external audit of the indirect or overhead percentage that is to be added to the direct time, and other factors of concern to the client.

Determination of fee is not simply a matter of determining the dollars of fee required. In addition, there is need to determine how the fee will be described in the contract documents, including the degree of flexibility in amount of fee to be paid if the amount of work varies from that anticipated. Some of the more commonly used types of fee structure include:

1. *Lump sum or firm fixed price (FFP).* With this type of fee, the consulting engineer is paid a fixed dollar amount which is negotiated for a described scope of services. This is simple to administer because there is a clear understanding of the amount of fee to be paid. It does, however, place significant risk on the consulting engineering firm because if the cost of the work required to perform the scope of services is higher than anticipated at the time the fee was negotiated, the consulting engineer bears the burden. If the scope changes, there would, of course, be a basis for renegotiation of fee.

2. *Percent of construction cost.* With this fee structure, the consulting engineer is paid an amount of dollars equal to a negotiated percentage of the cost of construction of the project designed. This type of fee is applicable only to services that are directly related to design and construction of a project. A major drawback is that the amount of consulting engineering services required on a project is not necessarily a function of the construction cost of the project. A major advantage of this type of fee structure has been its comparative simplicity and the fact that a percentage could be negotiated based on the general type of project without having to know the precise size and content of the project. Nevertheless, several U.S. government agencies have strongly discouraged use of this fee structure and its use is declining.

3. *Cost plus fixed fee (CPFF).* With this fee structure, the consulting engineer is paid the cost of providing the services (including direct time, direct expense, and indirect costs) plus a "fixed fee," which is a negotiated dollar amount intended to cover the risk of performing the services, any costs which are not allowed by the client in the buildup of "costs," income taxes, return on assets employed, and profit. A major advantage of this type of fee structure is that it allows a reasonable flexibility in scope of services. The scope does not have to be as precisely defined as it is in the case of FFP. With CPFF, the client pays the actual costs incurred (both direct and indirect) whether or not they differ from those estimated at the outset. The consulting engineer also receives the "fixed fee." Thus, the risk to the consulting engineer is somewhat less, but the consulting engineer retains an incentive to minimize costs incurred. In an effort to reduce their risk, some clients will insist on a ceiling or maximum total compensation to be paid to the consulting engineer. This usually poses no problem if the ceiling amount is set at least 15 to 25 percent above the total compensation estimated at the outset. However, if the ceiling is set closer to the actual estimated compensation, the risk to the consulting engineer increases and a lump sum fee would probably be more equitable.

4. *Hourly fee plus direct expenses.* Many consulting engineers establish hourly billing rates for various staff members. When these staff members work on a client engagement, the client is billed the appropriate hourly rate for the direct time charged. In addition, the client is billed for the actual direct expenses incurred in carrying out the engagement, perhaps with a modest markup to reimburse the consulting engineer for the accounting and handling of them. This fee structure is perhaps the most equitable. With it, the client pays for actual services rendered and the consulting engineer receives payment for what has been done. In addition, it is easily and simply administered. For these reasons, it is commonly used in private sector work, often with a ceiling or maximum dollar amount.

5. *Direct time times a multiplier plus direct expense.* This type of fee structure is a variation of the hourly fee plus expense. Rather than using established hourly fees for various staff members, the consulting engineer may charge the actual direct time cost times a multiplier, plus the direct expense incurred. As with the hourly-fee-plus-direct-expense structure, there may also be a modest markup on direct expenses. If hourly direct time costs are based on salary only, multipliers commonly range from 2.4 to 3.0. The advantages, disadvantages, and use of this fee structure are similar to those for the hourly-fee-plus-expenses structure. Again, a ceiling or maximum is often included.

6. *Other fee types.* Other types of fee structure are used from time to time. Many are a combination or a variation of the fee structures described above. For example, the consulting engineer may be paid a lump-sum compensation for some portions of the scope, and other portions may carry a compensation of hourly fees plus direct expenses. Some types of fee structure spell out certain elements of cost which are reimbursable, and the remainder is included under another type of fee structure. The possibilities for other types of fee structures are almost endless.

The type of fee structure most appropriate to a particular engagement depends on the characteristics of the engagement. How well-defined is the scope of services to be provided? Does the engagement entail services that are comparatively straightforward and not subject to surprises, or does it entail experimental or research effort which cannot be readily quantified? Inflexible fee structures such as lump sum are appropriate for straightforward situations where the scope is well defined. More flexible fee structures such as CPFF or hourly fee plus expenses are more appropriate where the scope is not so well defined, or where it is desired to minimize the time and cost involved in negotiating scope changes.

The criteria for selection of the best type of fee structure include simplicity, equity, and auditability. For a given situation, the fee structure should be one that can be administered as simply as possible. It should be one in which the risks are shared equitably between the client and the consulting engineer, and in which the billings to the client can be easily audited, following tracks left by the cost-accounting system of the consulting engineer.

Contract and Fee Negotiation

The objective of the contract and fee negotiation is to arrive at a mutually understood and acceptable statement of the scope and plan for the work, including the compensation to be paid to the consulting engineer. In a very real sense, the contract and fee negotiation process is a part of the planning of the engagement. Properly handled, it provides the best possible opportunity for thorough review of the scope of work to be done, the approaches to be used to do it, key project team assignments, schedule, and methodology. In such a negotiation, scope and work plan are primary and fee is derivative.

Often, the steps taken prior to contract and fee negotiation include a client audit of the consulting engineer's accounting system. Such an audit establishes many unit costs such as hourly payroll costs for applicable categories of staff members, overhead or indirect costs as a percentage of direct time costs, and unit costs for supporting services such as computer usage, printing, etc. With these unit costs established, the focus of contract and fee negotiations becomes one of determining the amount, type, and schedule of services to be provided. When these are agreed upon, the calculation of fee becomes primarily a matter of applying the audited cost rates to the agreed scope and plan.

For this reason, the most effective contract and fee negotiations usually are carried out by knowledgeable design professionals from the client and consulting engineer organizations. People knowledgeable in the work to be done and able to discuss alternatives and changes in approach can most effectively arrive at an optimal scope and, hence, fee.

Cash-Flow Management

The expenditures of a consulting engineering firm occur at a predictable and regular rate. They include salaries, payroll-related costs, rents, taxes, insurance, purchases, and similar elements. For the most part, all can be projected quite accurately. In contrast, receipts are less predictable. They are almost totally dependent on billings and collections from clients. For this reason, economic viability of a consulting engineering firm is significantly dependent on the firm's ability to manage its cash flow to provide receipts which are sufficient to meet expenditures.

The first step in cash-flow management is careful client selection. It makes no sense to work for clients who do not pay their bills. Therefore, an important part of the decision to enter into a contract with a particular client is the credit rating and reputation of that client for prompt payment of bills.

Secondly, cash receipts are greatly affected by the payment schedule and terms included in the negotiated professional services contracts. The consulting engineer should negotiate schedules for payment of fees that maintain the payments on a current basis. The precedent for progress payments is well established. The normal contract terms should provide that the consulting engineer is to be paid on at least a monthly basis in proportion to progress on the work. In addition, if the services being provided entail significant mobilization costs for a field task force or team, the payment schedule should provide for payment of these mobilization costs at a time approximating when they are incurred.

Equity suggests that the payment terms include significant penalties such as interest for late payment by the client. If the billings to the client are not paid in a timely fashion, the consulting engineer may have to resort to borrowing to meet ongoing expenditures. The client penalties for late payment of billings should therefore be set at a level high enough to more than cover the costs of borrowing.

A third step toward effective cash-flow management is careful attention to client billings. The consulting engineer should learn and understand the client's system for review, approval, and payment of billings. Billing dates should be established so that the time between receipt by the client and payment is minimized. The billing content and format should give the client all information needed for expeditious processing. Finally, those responsible for managing the client engagement should pay close attention to be sure that all billings are prompt and timely.

Once billings are submitted to the client, they will show up on the accounts receivable reports. They should then be monitored carefully for payment. Normally, it should not take longer than 30 days for a client to review and pay a billing. If a given billing goes beyond a normal payment time, follow-up is appropriate. This will ascertain if there are any particular problems with the billing and permit early corrective action. Following this, it may be appropriate to periodically remind the client of nonpayment. Reminder that the contract contains penalties for nonpayment may be an inducement to give the billing prompt attention. Ultimately, if a client does not pay legitimate billings, it may be necessary for the consulting engineer to threaten and then to stop work on the engagement. Nonpayment of justifiable billings is a breach of contract and legal action may ultimately be required. Clearly, collection efforts need to be handled judiciously and wisely. The client may be delaying payment because of some real or imagined concern about the progress of the work. Careful follow-up will ascertain the reasons for nonpayment and permit the consulting engineer to decide on the best strategy.

Effective cash-flow management permits the consulting engineering firm to minimize the working capital tied up in the business and maximize return on assets employed. Both short- and long-term cash-flow planning are effective tools in determining the amount of working capital required and the amount of short-term borrowing that may be necessary to finance the working capital. Typically, the collection period for billings for consulting engineering firms is in the range of 60 to 70 days, although collection periods as low as 30 to 40 days and as high as 90 to 100 days are not unknown. Each consulting engineering firm should endeavor to minimize its collection period to a level consistent with its practice and clientele. In addition, it should be certain that it maintains adequate working capital within the firm to finance the work in process and accounts receivable that it normally experiences.

Financing

A consulting engineering firm that is too thinly financed will have difficulty achieving economic viability. The assets employed in a practice range from 25 to 50 percent of the annual revenue of the firm. The average ratio of assets to revenues probably runs in the neighborhood of 40 percent. As this range of figures suggests, the amount of capital required in the business varies with the nature of the practice and clientele as well as the financial management philosophy and effectiveness.

One factor that greatly affects the amount of capitalization required is the extent to which the firm has elected to own or lease office, computer, and other major facilities. There are advantages and disadvantages to both ownership and leasing of such facilities. Over the long run, lease costs tend to be higher than ownership costs because the lessor must cover the ownership costs as well as make a profit on the facility. However, leased facilities require less capital and all lease costs are fully deductible as business-operating costs. The merits of lease versus ownership should be carefully analyzed before the firm commits to substantial facilities leases or investments.

The assets required to operate a consulting engineering firm must be financed from some combination of liabilities and net worth. Current liabilities, largely accounts and salaries payable, will seldom finance more than about one-third to one-half of the current assets of a firm. Consulting engineering firms do not have a tangible inventory that can be used as collateral for debt financing. Therefore, the primary bases for debt financing arise out of mortgage borrowing on facilities or short-term lines of credit secured only by the ongoing assets and historical financial performance of the practice.

For these reasons, the greater part of the capital required for operation of a consulting engineering firm is provided by the equity ownership or net worth of the firm. Typically, half or more of the total assets are financed by equity, rather than liabilities. However, the ratio of equity or net worth to total assets may run as low as 25 to 30 percent or as high as 75 to 80 percent.

Another aspect of financing, namely the source of equity, merits mention. The equity ownership of consulting engineering firms is most commonly held by a limited number of principals of the firm. One of the continuing problems of financial management is developing procedures whereby principals may reduce and divest ownership as they approach retirement. Correspondingly, the firm must develop procedures for acquisition of this equity ownership by the future principals and managers. Most firms that have developed effective patterns of ownership transition have done it by financing the transition out of the earnings of the firm. Clearly, effective ownership transition is essential to the continuity of the firm and, hence, an essential ingredient of economic success.

Risk Management

Economic viability also requires attention to risk management. At one level, risk management involves operation of the firm so as to limit to acceptable levels the risks taken on by the firm. There is no such thing as risk-free practice.

Risk management involves careful control of contract documents so that the firm does not take on responsibility for acts of others and accepts responsibility for its work which is not greater than that consistent with the practice of professional engineering. Risk management includes screening prospective clients to avoid those with unfortunate histories of disputes and litigation. It includes internal quality-control procedures to maintain high professional standards of work. It includes careful attention to client relations and engagement performance so as to be able to sense and correct any incipient difficulties. It includes monitoring political risks. It includes building a sound and stable practice which is strong enough to withstand reasonable adversity.

But, beyond this, each firm must determine which risks it can afford to carry and which can and should be insured. Nearly all consulting engineering firms carry professional liability insurance which, with appropriate deductibles, limits, etc., insures against errors and omissions arising out of the professional practice. Professional liability insurance is the most costly insurance carried by firms. The annual premium cost of such insurance typically ranges from 3 to 4.0 percent of gross billings for very small firms to 1.5 to 2.0 percent of gross billings for very large firms. The average premium cost is in the range of 2.5 to 3.0 percent of annual gross billings.

In addition, the firm may elect to carry political risk insurance on overseas work. It will certainly carry general liability, auto liability, worker's compensation, and other general business insurance. Most firms insure fringe-benefit programs such as group life and medical programs.

Effective risk management requires both internal attention and competent counsel and advice from outside the organization.

Conclusion

The economic viability of a consulting engineering firm requires both sound professional practice and effective business management. The probabilities of achieving both are enhanced by ownership and management of the firm by principals who are competent design professionals and also sensitive to the business needs of the practice.

Economic viability is measured by financial accounting reports and controlled by managerial accounting reports. Each person who is or would be a principal or manager of a consulting engineering firm must have a thorough understanding of the financial and managerial accounting system and reports used by the firm. Properly used, they form the basis for the managerial decisions that lead to economic success.

Maintenance of a satisfactory balance between workload and staff, competent planning and control of each client engagement, negotiation of a satisfactory professional services contract and fee for each engagement, management of cash flow, and adequate financing and risk management are essential parts of the economic well-being of a consulting engineering firm.

The young engineer who begins a career in consulting engineering practice is well advised to learn the elements of financial management, understand the management practices and procedures used by the firm, and develop professional capabilities in both engineering and management. Some highly successful consulting engineers focus their efforts primarily on their engineering endeavors. Others focus most heavily in engineering management. Both areas are essential parts of the economic viability of a consulting engineering practice.

Chapter

PROFESSIONAL RELATIONSHIPS

Eugene B. Waggoner
Consulting Engineering Geologist

By its very nature, the subject of professional relationships is a complex mixture of the philosophy of the profession and pragmatic response to the business environment that affects the profession. Professional relationships, in brief, are those personal and operational bonds or connections that exist between persons of high standards, experience, skill, and training in a specified vocation requiring mental rather than manual expertise, the vocation in this case being the practice of consulting engineering.

Until the early 1900s, when the American Institute of Consulting Engineers (AICE) was formed in New York, consulting engineers nationwide tended to be loners and to practice as individuals or single firms, each going its own way, each shying away from any formalized professional relationship. But by the early 1950s, consulting engineers, initially through association in technical societies, began to realize that their competitors were really not much different from themselves, that they had many important mutual interests, and that many of these interests would be furthered more effectively by community actions. The result was the creation in 1956 of the Consulting Engineers Council (CEC) of the United States. In 1973 AICE joined with CEC to form the present American Consulting Engineers Council (ACEC).

The value of coming together as a national community is exemplified in the strength and growth of ACEC and of today's practice of consulting engineering. Today, consulting engineers meet together and share both technical and business experiences. They agree to adhere to a common set of business and professional ethics.

141

They act together politically, contribute jointly to public service and benefit, and work together on projects too large for individuals or single firms. They also try to police their own profession for the benefit of their clients, and acting as a community of professionals, they are gaining public visibility. The public has become aware that the consulting engineer is at the forefront of, and is intimately involved in some way with, almost every aspect of present-day living. They are involved with the design and construction of where we live and where we work, the development of our resources and energy, the distribution of water, the transportation of our goods and ourselves, the design of facilities for defense and the protection of our environment. The list could continue, encompassing as many as 200 consulting engineering specialties.

No statement about the community of consulting engineers would be complete without pointing out its importance to the engineer from a minority background. The greatest opportunity for these engineers to become entrepreneurs lies in their chance to own or share ownership in a business that has great public visibility and recognition, such as the practice of consulting engineering. Formerly, the principal opportunity for minority engineers lay almost solely in the academic or government areas, or in being employees of a nonminority engineering firm. But this has not been sufficient to induce many minority students to enter the engineering profession. In the last few years, however, minority engineers have found that they can enter and compete in the private practice field, and that they are being recognized as an important part of it. Government agencies at all levels have recognized the importance of minorities in private practice and are stimulating their entry into the field by requiring minority participation in practically all major publicly-funded projects.

Acceptance of minority engineering firms is on the same basis as acceptance of new nonminority firms. Each firm is expected to live by the established rules or guidelines for practice and to succeed or fail upon the quality of its services and ability to manage its business efficiently. That the minority engineering firms are succeeding is testified to by the growth in the number of such firms and their inclusion with nonminority firms in many joint ventures, subcontracts, and full participating associations.

The Ethics of the Profession

In the practice of engineering, consulting engineers and engineers in other fields have developed codes of ethics and/or rules of practice through their professional and technical associations and societies. In general, the codes and rules are similar, with the nonconsulting groups' codes somewhat less oriented towards business practice.

In the consulting engineering community, codes of ethics apply not only to relationships between engineers, but to behavior towards clients and the public. In reality, these codes are not strict statements of moral beliefs but are standards of practice that engineers have agreed to follow. They are designed to eliminate activities that would be unfair or damaging to others in the profession, and to protect the interests of the public and the client.

The American Consulting Engineers Council publishes an ethical code called The Professional and Ethical Conduct Guidelines. Given here are its Preamble and Fundamental Canons*:

PREAMBLE

Consulting engineering is an important and learned profession. The members of the profession recognize that their work has a direct and vital impact on the quality of life for all people. Accordingly, the services provided by consulting engineers require honesty, impartiality, fairness and equity and must be dedicated to the protection of the public health, safety and welfare. In the practice of their profession, consulting engineers must perform under a standard of professional behavior which requires adherence to the highest principles of ethical conduct on behalf of the public, clients, employees and the profession.

I. Fundamental Canons
   Consulting engineers, in the fulfillment of their professional duties, shall:
   1. Hold paramount the safety, health and welfare of the public in the performance of their professional duties.
   2. Perform services only in areas of their competence.
   3. Issue public statements only in an objective and truthful manner.

---

*The complete Professional and Ethical Conduct Guidelines enlarge upon these canons in detail; copies can be obtained from ACEC's central office at 1015 15th Street NW, Washington, D.C. 20005.

4. Act in professional matters for each client as faithful agents or trustees.
5. Avoid improper solicitation of professional assignments.

Interrelationships among Firms

Although not all consulting engineers are members of an organized group of engineering consultants, many individuals and firms belong to one or more groups, ranging from local to state to national organizations. These organizations or associations can be either technical or professional societies where membership is by individuals, or business practice–oriented associations, where membership is by firms rather than by individuals. We are concerned primarily here with the latter group, for this is where relationships between firms are most easily and frequently developed. ACEC is an example of a large and effective business practice–oriented association of consulting engineers.

The interrelationships between consulting engineering firms are many—some simple, some complex. They range from social relationships through every phase of business operations and into political action groups. The relationships predominantly spring from two areas: the first, activities connected with engineering associations; the second, those that various firms work out between themselves in the practice of their business.

Most relationships pursued through associations consist of membership and service together on committees or in governmental affairs presentations. The joint action of firms working together on committees has produced business forms, documents, and procedures used in daily business practice, such as basic manuals of practice, standardized forms for contract documents, arbitration procedures, professional liability and loss abatement programs, minority affairs guidance, building codes and standards, international engineering liaison, engineering education and scholarship programs, and engineering environmental protection programs.

The business relationships that firms work out between themselves include subcontracts, architect-engineer arrangements, joint ventures, and other kinds of project agreements or associations.

Subcontracts

One of the basic rules of engineering practice is that one should not seek or attempt to perform services beyond one's area of competence. With some 200 or more consulting engineering specialties and many projects that require several of these different specialties or disciplines, a firm may find a need to augment its staff temporarily with an individual specialist or specialty firm to serve special needs of a client. It is not unusual for a general civil engineering design firm to require the services of a geotechnical, electrical, mechanical, or structural consulting firm, for example, to perform most of their services by subcontract rather than by serving as a prime consultant.

Architect-Engineer Relationships

At one time, most major projects were conceived, designed, and supervised by architects or architectural firms. Engineering was subcontracted by the architect to engineering firms; the architect served as the prime professional and made all contact with the client. As projects grew in size and complexity, the proportion of engineering to architecture became larger to the point where more engineering than architectural services were required on some projects. This led to discord in the relationships between architects and engineers, with the accompanying contract arguments over fees, responsibilities for supervision, and overlapping technical input. The result was that more consulting engineers sought the prime role in designing and supervising projects. Other consulting engineers sought separate direct contracts with clients rather than subcontracts with architects. In other instances, architects added engineers to their firms and engineers added architectural staffs, creating what is referred to as architect-engineer (A-E) firms. Individuals and small engineering firms in special disciplines now may choose to subcontract to architectural firms, to other consulting engineering firms, to A-E firms, or directly to a client.

To accommodate these various approaches to practice, standard subcontract forms were developed primarily by joint committees of architects and consulting engineers. Such cooperative efforts have brought about a better understanding of each others' capabilities and professional standards and resulted in mutual respect and easier working relationships.

Joint Ventures

A business enterprise in which there is some danger of loss as well as a chance for profit is a venture. When that venture is shared with someone else it is a joint venture. In consulting engineering, a joint venture is created when two or more consulting engineering firms agree to act as a single entity in seeking a contract to perform engineering services on a project. A joint venture differs from a partnership in that it is formed to carry out a single project rather than to serve as an ongoing business relationship.

There are a number of reasons why firms may want to act as a joint venture: the volume of work may be more than any of the individual firms can accomplish in the allotted time; the range of services required may not exist in one firm alone; or the assumption of the project may induce a cash-flow problem that one firm could not handle. The professional liability risks also may be more than a single firm would be able to assume and, if bonding or insurance is required, it may be more than any of the participating firms could obtain alone. Sometimes the participating firms decide they would rather have a part of a project than risk losing it all by competing for it alone; sometimes a client may want a local firm for the project, but that local firm may need the help of a larger, more experienced firm from another city.

Whatever the reason for the joint venture, it behooves the participants to step as carefully in setting up the venture as in performing the services. No joint venture should be entered into without the assistance of an attorney who is qualified and experienced in such contracts. The prospective venturers should know each other well—their strengths and weaknesses, their respective past records in similar ventures, their financial backgrounds, and their technical competence and staff strength. Joint venturing means sharing the work fairly, sharing the costs of doing the work, risking a loss rather than a profit, and being willing to share liability for the other firm's errors, omissions, or negligence as well as one's own. If the participating firms have different insurance companies, those companies must agree on the terms of a joint insurance policy, or the project may be excluded from coverage. Usually a special insurance policy is designed for the joint venture. When the joint venture obtains the project, all parties must be in agreement as to which people will manage it, how the work will be divided, who will be the contact with the client, and how the accounting will be set up. Finally, agreement must be reached on how profits and losses are to be shared.

Two types of joint ventures are unusually risky: one in which the consulting engineering firm enters into a joint venture with a contractor on a turnkey project, and one in which the firm joint-ventures with an owner in what amounts to a contingency type of project. (The joint venture with a contractor, however, is quite common on large international projects, where circumstances vary widely from those of domestic practice.)

In such joint ventures a consulting engineering firm may find itself in the position of having to cut corners or of approving unsatisfactory material or workmanship. This could create a serious liability situation and many insurers will not cover their engineer-clients for these kinds of joint venture.

Project Associations

Strictly speaking, these are informal associations in which one or more firms work on the same project for the same client, each firm performing the services of its own discipline. Each participating firm is solely and only responsible or liable for its own work. None of the associated firms is supervised by any other, and each supervises or inspects the construction or performance of the work it has designed or specified. Such associations usually come about as the result of certain firms finding they work together amicably and efficiently. Because of this, they recommend each other to their respective clients when the project requires services they cannot perform themselves. In other instances, a project owner selects the team of different firms he wants, makes a separate contract with each firm, and then instructs them to work together in an informal project association. Where the participating firms seek and arrange their own associations for projects, there is less risk of interfirm conflict than when the owner creates the association and instructs them to work together.

Professional Engineer (P.E.) Registration

The practice of engineering in the United States is legally recognized as affecting the welfare and safety of the general public. As a result, state legislatures have enacted laws to regulate the licensing of engineers (and land surveyors) in their respective states. The engineering practice acts of the divers states have a similar purpose although they vary considerably in their requirements. The generally stated purpose of licensing or registration is "to safeguard life, health, and property and to promote the public welfare." Each state establishes a board of registration to administer the registration requirements and procedures and to monitor the members of the profession to see that they comply with registration laws. It is not the intent here to describe in detail the engineer-registration laws of each state, but only to indicate what some of the differences are. The student planning to go into the practice of engineering should contact the state or states in which he intends to practice to learn their respective requirements for licensing. In most states the student first must go through an engineering internship as an engineer in training (EIT). After completion of the EIT requirements, the student may apply for a professional engineer's (P.E.) license. Most states require examinations for the EIT and the P.E.

Some states recognize licensing from another state, or grant a license on "eminence" or oral examination alone; in some, an engineer who works for a governmental agency, for industry, or under the supervision of a licensed engineer need not be registered. The engineer who has received the P.E. license is given an official seal that must be put on his work, or on that of unlicensed subordinates. Misuse of the seal may result in license revocation.

Registration may be simply as a professional engineer with no indication of discipline specialty, or it may be mandatory to be classified in some basic discipline, such as civil, structural, electrical, or mechanical. States that have a "title act" permit further breakdown into very specialized fields of engineering. A "title act" registration is one that requires any person who uses a specified title, such as quality engineer, safety engineer, etc., to be registered with the state board and to meet the board's requirements for such registration by examination and/or other means. Title registration only protects use of the title. A Mandatory Practice Act registration protects the use of the title and, more important, requires an individual to be registered if he offers his services to the public.

Because most clients are lay persons and the purpose of registration is to safeguard the public, boards of registration include members drawn from the lay public as well as from the ranks of the profession.

From time to time we hear complaints about the concept of licensing engineers, that it creates unneeded little bureaucracies or restrains the right to practice. For the most part, however, the profession believes strongly in registration and believes it functions well in protecting the public. Requiring licensing by registration places a responsibility directly on the individual engineer to qualify to practice. In accepting and using the seal, the engineer is publicly stating a personal responsibility for the work he has signed.

Groupings for Large Projects

In the last several years the nation's problems with development, energy and natural resources, waste management, water treatment, transportation of people and goods, and facilities for national defense have grown formidably. This growth has spawned a corresponding need for large-scale projects to handle these problems. Local, state, and federal government agencies and private industry are conceiving and calling for construction of such large projects that single firms and even small groups of engineering firms cannot accomplish them in the desired time. This has brought about what is called a consortium. It generally consists of several firms, including all of the required disciplines, the people to staff the project, and the necessary financial resources. A consortium for a single project would be a large joint venture; if for more than one project, it would be a partnership.

The administration and operation of these consulting engineering consortia throughout the project, which may take many years to complete, become very complex. If not planned and executed properly from the beginning, they can become a maze of paperwork, meetings, and organizational delays. Experienced and knowledgeable administrators, as well as experienced and capable engineers, are essential to keep these large groups operating efficiently. Examples of projects calling for such large groupings of engineers would be major city rapid-transit systems, large nuclear power developments, major defense installations, and space research programs.

Technical Papers and Exchange of Information

Exchange of technical information is a matter of vital importance to every profession, and the engineering profession is no exception. It is particularly important to the practice of consulting engineering because it is a front-line area of the profession, a way in which the engineer may keep up with the current state of the art. When the quality of an engineer's work is being examined, the first question asked is, "Was it performed in accordance with the current state of the art?" To answer this question in the affirmative, the engineer must not only know basic engineering, but what is new in engineering, how it is done, how well it works, and when to apply it. To avoid obsolescence, the engineer must exchange new knowledge and experience with others in his profession. There are a number of ways this can be done. The most common form of written technical communication is that of technical papers published in technical and professional magazines. Some of the publications are organs of the various technical societies, others are magazines such as *Consulting Engineer,* which are not aligned with any society and publish business and professional articles as well as technical material. Technical articles may be included in the proceedings and special papers prepared for meetings, seminars, workshops, and lectures. Papers written by consulting engineers usually include abundant case-history information and analyses of why some engineering project functioned exceptionally well or another did not.

Oral communication usually takes place through meetings, seminars, lectures, and workshops. Consulting engineers frequently serve as special lecturers at universities and colleges.

Technical knowledge may be exchanged visually by visits to projects either completed or under construction. Such visits may be by a few engineers or by large groups in a formal field trip. Most field trips are coincident with a general meeting of some engineering organization.

Governmental entities are another channel of communications. A government agency that has a direct engineering function will issue public reports on its projects or research. Other agencies may purchase engineering services or sponsor engineering research. These agencies select consulting engineering firms and educational organizations to perform services and research, and this work and research ultimately is written up and published by the agencies.

Although this discussion is primarily related to the exchange of technical information in the United States, it is important to note that in the engineering profession, and particularly in the consulting engineering field, there is a strong line of international communications. This exchange is through publications and by personal contact through international organizations such as International Commission on Large Dams (ICOLD), International Commission on Irrigation and Drainage (ICID), and the International Federation of Consulting Engineers (FIDIC).

THE INTERNATIONAL MARKET

Joseph C. Lawler
Chairman of the Board, Camp Dresser & McKee, Inc.

Work in developing countries poses a far greater challenge to consulting engineers than does work under the familiar conditions of the United States. The challenge is many-faceted, ranging from the social and political significance of such assignments to the multiple problems associated with working far from the home office, in strange surroundings, amid people of a different culture. The client's personnel are often technically unsophisticated, but understandably reluctant to acknowledge the fact; facilities are limited, and the technological resources of the area usually are minimal. Thus the role of the consulting engineer working in a developing country often embraces a much wider scope and has a much greater impact on the area than would a similar assignment in an industrialized country. The remoteness and the communication problems posed by distance and less-than-adequate facilities require engineers in the field to rely more heavily on their own knowledge, ingenuity, decision-making capacity, and ability to relate to people than when they are working in a familiar environment. For those who can meet the challenge, an overseas assignment is an opportunity for growth and fulfillment; for others, it is a source of frustration and defeat.

Potential Foreign Engineering Work

Work available to U.S. consultants in the developed countries outside the United States is limited. It is, for the most part, either of highly specialized character performed by individuals as a purely consulting service, or more frequently, it is provided to U.S.-based industrial clients by their customary consulting firms or by design-construct organizations with an established reputation for work in the particular industry. Because such work is only of passing interest to those to whom this volume is particularly directed, discussion in this chapter will be limited to work in the developing countries.

The size of that market is difficult to estimate. Indicative of its magnitude is a 1980 survey by *Engineering News-Record* in cooperation with the University of Florida's School of Building Construction. The survey found that, collectively, the top 150 consulting firms of all nationalities responding to the survey had 1979 foreign billings (i.e., billings for work outside their own countries) totaling $2.1 billion. This included work in the developed countries. Allowing for this, and for billings of those consultants who worked abroad but either were not reached in the survey or failed to respond, it is estimated that the 1979 developing-country market for consulting engineering services was at least $2 billion. United States consultants claimed approximately 38 percent of the total, followed by British firms with 15 percent, French 9 percent, Canadians 7 percent, and Dutch 4 percent; consultants from 13 other countries accounted for the remaining 17 percent. The survey listed 78 U.S. firms among the top 150 engaged in work outside their own borders. The large share reported by U.S. firms, and the fact that the survey was conducted by a U.S. organization, may indicate less than complete coverage of foreign consultants and hence a larger actual total market.

The richest market area in 1979 was the middle east, where Saudi Arabia provided almost half the work. Africa, paced by Egypt, Nigeria, and Algeria, was second; Latin America third; and the far east, led by the Philippines and Indonesia, fourth. Iran, formerly one of the most active areas for overseas consulting assignments, is currently out of the market for all practical purposes, and future prospects there are uncertain. India and China have enormous potential, but penetration of those markets will be difficult. India has substantial engineering resources of its own and at present makes only limited use of foreign consultants. Of the 150 top firms in the *ENR*-University of Florida survey, only 12 that responded worked in India. Of these, 4 were from the United States and 4 were British. China has great need and desire for Western technology but little foreign exchange to pay for it. However, China recently joined the

World Bank, which may improve consulting opportunities there. The prospects for U.S. consulting engineers are somewhat dimmed by the U.S. government which, for purposes of foreign policy, has offered the services of the Army Corps of Engineers and TVA for hydroelectric developments, flood control, and river and harbor improvement work. Nonetheless, the Corps has stated publicly that it does not intend to shut private consultants out of major opportunities in China.

An analysis of Inter-American Development Bank loans made to Latin American countries in 1978 is of interest as an indication of the types of work available to consultants in the developing countries. IDB loans that year for various purposes totaled $1.9 billion and covered approximately a third of the total cost of the projects financed. The distribution by sector was as follows:

Energy, principally electric power	41 %
Industry and mining	17 %
Agriculture, including irrigation	13 %
Transportation and communication	10 %
Water supply and sanitation	8 %
Other	11 %

Competitive Position of U.S. Consultants Abroad

The quality of U.S. engineering and the ethical standards of U.S. consulting engineers are widely known and appreciated abroad. These positive competitive factors are offset by the relatively high cost of U.S. engineering and by growing competition from others who enjoy various forms of financial support from their governments that are not provided by ours. Nevertheless, U.S. citizens continue to be a major presence in the overseas engineering market, though their share is declining.

A number of factors adversely affect the competitive position of U.S. consultants. Cost is one of these, particularly as foreign clients, always faced with limited budgets and foreign exchange problems, have become highly cost-conscious and are resorting increasingly to consideration of price, if not of actual competitive bidding, in the selection process. United States costs are influenced greatly by the burdens imposed by our federal government. United States citizens working abroad are subject to the same personal income tax schedules faced by those working at home, and their effect is intensified by substantially higher overseas taxable income. United States firms must pay higher salaries for foreign employment to induce Americans to accept the isolation, unfamiliar environment, more difficult living conditions, and other problems associated with work in developing countries. Further, Americans are required to treat as taxable income many of the allowances necessarily provided in the normal overseas employment agreement, including housing and living costs, children's educational expenses, and home-leave travel costs.

While overseas employment salary exclusions in some instances provide a measure of relief, the overseas employee generally finds himself in a substantially higher tax bracket than if he were doing similar work at home. Personal income taxes paid to the host country government may also be a problem, particularly when they are based on a sliding scale that may be reasonable when applied to the income levels prevalent in the country but confiscatory with respect to the much higher earnings of foreigners. To the extent that such taxes cannot be used to offset U.S. tax obligations or alleviated by provisions in the engineering firm's contract, they must be compensated for in the firm's contracts with its employees and reflected in its charges to the client.

The United States is believed to be the only government of a competing country that taxes the income which its citizens earn outside its territory. Many of our competitors' countries recognize that construction contracts and exports tend to follow engineering and therefore assist their engineers' foreign sales efforts with strong diplomatic mission support and by subsidizing the pursuit of new overseas assignments.

Funding Overseas Projects

The economic situations of the non-oil-exporting developing countries require external grants or borrowing to finance the foreign exchange costs of their projects. Grants and loans are provided directly by many of the developed countries, who also provide the capital for the great international lending agencies. Direct grants and loans are usually "tied," that is, they contain a requirement that external expenditures made from them go, with some exceptions, to the country supplying the funds. The United States provides direct grants and credits for economic development through AID, a component of the International Development Cooperation Agency (IDCA). These are partially tied funds. United States commercial banks provide substantial funds to foreign governments for all purposes, including development, and at the end of 1978 had outstanding loans to the developing countries totaling nearly $28 billion.

The major sources of untied loans for economic development projects of interest to engineers are:

The International Bank for Reconstruction and Development (World Bank)

The Inter-American Development Bank (IDB)

The Asian Development Bank

The African Development Bank

The United Nations Development Programme (UNDP)

The World Health Organization

The Food and Agriculture Organization

In general, the major oil-exporting countries are able to finance both the foreign exchange and local currency requirements of their development projects out of oil revenues and do not resort to borrowing.

Engineers considering a specific overseas assignment should be aware of the source of funding. A tied loan or grant will determine whether the work is available to U.S. firms alone or to engineers of some other country. The source of funds also influences the engineer selection procedure and sometimes the contract terms; it affects the manner and timing of payments, and it enables the engineer to better estimate the financial risk involved should he win the project.

Detailed information concerning the listed international agencies and others is contained in the *Consulting Engineers Guide to International Agencies,* published by the International Federation of Consulting Engineers (FIDIC). The pamphlet also lists other FIDIC publications of use to engineers interested in overseas assignments. Copies may be obtained from:

FIDIC Secretariat
P. O. Box 17334
2517 ES
The Hague
The Netherlands

The price is 5 Swiss francs, plus mailing costs. Overseas orders will be sent via boat mail unless airmail is specifically requested.

The World Bank issues a booklet entitled *Uses of Consultants by the World Bank and Its Borrowers.* It may be obtained without charge by writing to:

Office of Consulting Services Officer
The World Bank
1818 H Street, N. W.
Washington, D. C. 20006

The other development banks have generally similar rules concerning the use of consultants.

Government Support of Consultants

As has been noted, the competitive position of U.S. consulting engineers in the overseas market has suffered from U.S. personal income tax policy with respect to U.S. citizens working abroad. It also is adversely affected by the Foreign Corrupt Practices Act, the Antiboycott Act, and incentives provided for the competition by their governments, none of which tax their citizens on income earned outside the country. Many foreign governments also subsidize their engineering firms' new business activities abroad, stimulating their pursuit of foreign assignments and reducing their overhead charges.

Faced with an accumulated trade deficit of $95 billion during the decade of the 1970s, the U.S. government is now making increased efforts to expand the nation's exports, including the export of engineering and construction services. The International Trade Administration of the Department of Commerce collects information on engineering opportunities worldwide, and publishes these in the *Commerce Business Daily* and in a biweekly journal, *Business America*.

United States Foreign Service personnel are stationed in every country with which the United States maintains diplomatic relations. When in the area, engineers prospecting for work in such countries may contact them for information on proposed projects there, local laws, customs, and tax policies, and for introduction to local officials. United States embassies and consulates have improved their efforts to assist U.S. business executives abroad in recent years and are more useful sources of help than they had been in the past.

The International Development Cooperation Agency was recently formed as an independent government establishment to coordinate U.S. overseas development activities. It includes the Agency for International Development (AID), the Overseas Private Investment Corporation (OPIC), and the Trade and Development Program (TDP). The latter is of particular interest to engineers as a sponsor of such project-planning operations as project-identification missions, prefeasibility and feasibility studies, technological orientation missions for host government officials, and technical orientation symposia. The program provides financial support for feasibility studies for projects that can be financed by developing countries and undertaken by U.S. private industry or government agencies, including the Corps of Engineers. This program is relatively new and not yet adequately funded, but it is a promising step in the right direction, providing seed money for engineering services to stimulate the export of U.S. goods and services.

Political Risks

Political risks in the developing countries, although real, have often been shrugged off or completely disregarded by engineers beguiled by the prospect of an attractive contract. Risks arise from a variety of events, including political upheaval, insurrection, war, expropriation, currency fluctuations, convertibility, repatriation of profits, and contract disputes, in which the client holds the high cards because it controls the payments.

Assessment of risk is an imprecise science at best and is particularly difficult for the engineer, who lacks the information-gathering and evaluating capacity provided by a staff of experts in the field. Engineers must do the best they can using information gathered from U.S. Foreign Service personnel on the spot, local business people who are knowledgeable, U.S. bank branch managers in the area and, in the case of work financed by one of the international lending agencies, contacts in that organization. Political risk insurance is sometimes available from OPIC, a U.S. government operation, and from a few private underwriters, but no policy can cover the entire exposure. One of the best protections is a carefully drawn contract, with payment guaranteed by an irrevocable letter of credit drawn on a U.S. bank, but even that carries risk since payments must be approved by the responsible host country official.

Local Representation and Associates

When working in a foreign country, it is generally advantageous, and frequently required, to make use of a local associate either as a subconsultant or as a joint venture partner. There are numerous reasons for such an association. A secondary objective of many projects and the common desire of governments of developing countries is the transfer of technology and the upgrading of local technical resources. Association of a local consultant with the project is consistent with this objective and is a plus factor in client-consultant relations. The local associate's familiarity with host country laws, regulations, and conditions is of great value, and his knowledge of the highways and byways of local administration helps to get things done. He can usually supply the surveying, drafting, routine design, and supporting staff as part of a going organization at a much lower cost than if those services were provided by the foreign (U.S. or other) consultant.

Selection of the proper local associate is critical. Choosing a good one can help greatly, not only in winning the contract but in carrying it out: an incompetent or uncooperative associate is a heavy burden, a drag on job progress, and a constant source of friction and frustration. It is prudent, therefore, to make a thorough investigation of the possible candidates.

Names of local consulting firms may be obtained from a number of sources, including the local consulting engineers association, the commercial attaché of the U.S. Embassy, U.S. or other foreign consultants who are working or have worked in the country, and the local government planning and development agencies. Each of the possible candidates should be carefully evaluated, with selection based on these factors, among others:

Desire to participate in the project

Compatibility and ethics

Relevant prior experience and past performance

Ability to provide needed personnel

Facilities available for the associate's part of the work

Interest in seeking joint work on a continuing basis

Good reputation with the client

Independence from manufacturers and construction contractors

With an eye to the future, the candidate's willingness to develop a continuing relationship for the pursuit of additional work is an important consideration to the engineer who wishes to build an overseas business. All of the factors listed should be explored through visits to candidates' offices, discussions with the principals, and inquiries to previous clients of the candidate, government officials, and others who might provide information.

Local agents are a prerequisite to consideration for assignments in about half of the developing countries. They are a mixed blessing. If knowledgeable, discreet, motivated, reputable, and equipped with suitable office facilities, they can be very helpful and valuable. Some of those offering such service, unfortunately, are more interested in fees than in service, and these are of little use beyond satisfying the requirement for an agent.

There is always a temptation to employ a local agent on a retainer to cover a country or an area, keep the firm name before possible clients, funnel information on prospective work to the home office, and assist in the presentation of proposals. What has been said earlier in this chapter concerning required agents applies equally to such representatives. The best results gained from local representation usually come from capable local associates known from previous projects, who have a genuine incentive to develop new business because they expect to share in it.

Feasibility and Preinvestment Studies

Feasibility and preinvestment studies in the developing countries provide the engineer with the opportunity to develop a complete project concept based on terms of reference prepared jointly by the client and the international funding agency.

The titles "feasibility" and "preinvestment" adequately describe the purpose of such studies but give only a hint of the work required to carry them out. They can, and often do, involve surveys and the collection and development of basic data; the selection and preliminary design of alternative solutions; the assessment of their environmental impacts and their economic and social benefits; the selection of the optimum plan, with cost estimates for construction, operation and maintenance; and the preparation of a detailed report with recommendations. The report will be used to determine feasibility and, if favorable, to secure financing for the project and to guide the final design.

Feasibility and preinvestment studies are invariably prepared onsite because of the need for ready and continuous access to local information, the ability to make best use of the local associate, and the advantages of ready access to the client. Important studies usually require participation of a broad spectrum of disciplines, ranging from surveyors, geologists and agronomists, engineers, planners, geotechnical experts, and architects to ecologists and financial analysts. Disciplines and skills not available to the consultant in-house are obtained through subcontracts.

Design and Services during Construction

Design and the preparation of specifications for projects in the developing countries are often done on-site, in part because of client insistence, and in part for the same reasons that feasibility and preinvestment studies are done on-site. It is often possible to do part of the design and/or specification work in the home office, and the possibility should be explored since it may offer economies for both the engineer and the client. This option is most likely to be acceptable to the client on the more complex projects. It is desirable in some instances to bring client's personnel or key members of the local associate's staff to the home office to participate in project design work being done there, with both transfer-of-technology and client relations benefits.

Transfer of technology is also facilitated by regularly scheduled technical lectures by members of the engineer's local staff to local associate and client personnel. Close liaison between the overseas operation and the home office is essential to expedite design work, maintain quality, and keep costs within budget. Adequate computer facilities are not often available in developing country locations, and where computer analysis or design is required, it is usually performed in the home office, sometimes with the participation of engineers on the staff of the local associate or of the client.

Engineering services during construction are necessary on every construction project and are an absolute essential on work in the developing countries. They include assistance in obtaining and evaluating proposals and awarding contracts; examination of shop drawings; inspection of materials and equipment during manufacture, prior to shipment, and after receipt; inspection of the work during construction or installation to ensure compliance with contract requirements; interpretation of plans and specifications; provision of instructions to meet changed conditions and development of appropriate charge orders; monitoring of contractors' progress; checking and recommendation of contractors' requisitions for payment; maintenance of detailed job records and as-built drawings; performance of final inspections and preparation of acceptance recommendations; assistance in putting the work into successful operation; arbitration of disputes; and provision of a miscellaneous assortment of services necessary for the satisfactory completion of a successful project. Periodic reports to the client to keep him abreast of project progress, costs, present or anticipated problems, needed client decisions, and financial requirements are a necessary part of the chief resident engineer's duties.

Services during construction are best provided by the design engineer because of his familiarity with the work. They may be included in the design contract or may be made the subject of a separate agreement. In either case, the contract should be carefully drawn to define the engineer's duties and authority, the limits of his responsibility, and the basis of charges for his services. With rare exceptions, lump-sum contracts for this part of the work should be avoided since the engineer has little control over actual progress and the time his staff must spend on the job.

Services during construction usually are provided by an experienced chief resident engineer and a cadre of expatriate construction engineers provided by the consultant, with the supporting staff of junior engineers, inspectors, drafters, and clerical personnel supplied by the local associate, the client, or both. All are responsible to the chief resident engineer. The size of the staff and its makeup depend on the magnitude and complexity of the project. When selecting the chief resident engineer and his key staff members, the engineer should keep in mind that the success of the project, his relations with the client, and his reputation rest ultimately on their performance. The chief resident engineer must be more than a competent construction man. Because he stands between client and contractors, with a foot in both camps, he must have a judicial temperament, a well-developed ability to work with people, and the courage to enforce contract requirements equitably against contractor and client, buyer and seller alike.

Managerial and Operating Personnel Training

The lack of trained managerial, operating, and maintenance personnel is a major problem in the developing countries. In earlier years, when technology-based facilities in the third world were few, small, and simple, it was customary to operate them with a largely expatriate staff which was expected to train and use local workers in subordinate positions, but to retain control of all functions requiring technical skills. That practice is changing as facilities increase in number and sophistication and overseas governments become more aware of the need to develop the competence of their nationals. Governments of developing countries now tend to require that engineers and construction contractors not only design and build, but also train the work force needed to operate the facility. The training requirement may be included in the engineer's contract for design, or it may be the subject of a separate contract. In either case, the contract provisions should be specific as to the level of responsibility the engineer is expected to carry in the training program—whether general guidance or full responsibility—the class or classes of personnel to be trained, the training schedule timewise, the facilities to be provided by each party, the budget, and the engineer's basis of charges for the training program.

Before entering contract negotiations on or including a training program, the engineer should ascertain as nearly as possible what the client has in mind. The preproposal meeting, if held, would be an appropriate forum for inquiry. He should also develop his own ideas as to what is required, an outline of a suitable program, and an estimate of its probable cost. Intelligent front-end planning based on a thorough understanding of the needs and the human resources of the country and of the costs, time, and problems associated with meeting them are primary requisites of a successful training plan.

A detailed, bilingual operation and maintenance manual may be required as part of the design contract, particularly for a process facility or one including other than the simplest of machinery. The time and cost of preparing such a manual will vary with the size and complexity of the work, and problems are apt to arise in translation, since the language of the country may be deficient in technical terminology. Time and cost are easily underestimated by the engineer who has not had recent experience in manual preparation, and expert advice should be obtained when necessary. Preparation of such manuals may be subcontracted, but the design engineer should be an active participant in it.

Personnel for Overseas Work

The expense of sending personnel overseas and returning them to their home bases on completion of their assignments is an important element of project cost and justifies more than ordinary care in their selection. A successful track record on one or more jobs is an excellent recommendation. Individuals should be technically competent self-starters and able to operate under adverse conditions with a minimum of supervision. Ability to adapt to a foreign environment and a different culture, ingenuity, patience, and persistence also are assets. In most instances, it is inadvisable to send married persons on long foreign assignments without their spouses. If the spouse is to accompany an employee, willingness to go abroad and ability to adjust to the expected living conditions are important factors to be considered.

By far the best source of people for overseas work is the engineer's own staff. These are persons whose capabilities are known, who are familiar with the home office routine, its people and its sources of information, and who usually have an investment of years of service with the firm to protect and increase. The characteristics given above apply equally to selection of candidates from this source as they do to new employees hired in the open market. New employees should be thoroughly investigated by interview and by inquiry. Claimed degrees should be verified and all references checked, preferably by telephone or face-to-face conversation prior to making a commitment. Some employers have been badly deceived by neglecting to investigate thoroughly.

American firms in the past have tended to prefer U.S. citizens for their foreign operations, from familiarity and habit as much as for any other reason, but salary rates, benefits, and income tax equalization problems have changed this attitude markedly. European engineers are equally competent and may well be considered after carefully checking references and qualifications. Engineers other than Europeans are also being utilized in increasing numbers by U.S. firms. Locating suitable candidates is a problem that may be best approached through contact with the various national engineering associations in the countries of choice or through available area employment agencies. These agencies also assist in the important screening process and are acquainted with going salary rates.

There are numerous risks associated with hiring local staff in the host country. For this reason it is best to depend on the local associate to supply all local help. This also avoids complications arising out of local employment rules, the provisions and impact of which should be looked into and fully understood before engaging local employees.

Personnel Problems Overseas

Servicing requirements for personnel stationed in a developing country are greater by an order of magnitude than those for similar staff in the home office. Families are often involved, and so the problems range from such things as securing work permits and local professional registration to providing purely personal services. Even getting salary checks promptly to overseas employees requires special arrangements. Personal services for overseas employees are an important element in maintaining morale by reducing the inevitable sense of isolation that develops with time spent abroad. Serious illness of the employee or a member of his family is a problem, since good medical care is scarce and hospital service rudimentary or nonexistent in most third world countries.

Despite careful screening, employees or dependents sometimes prove unsuitable by temperament to live and work abroad, and make it necessary to repatriate them. Such instances are rare, as are cases of technical weakness or of personal incompatibility with the client's representative leading to a request for a substitution, but they do occur. Unstable political conditions in the host country sometimes make it necessary to evacuate the expatriate staff, and plans for such an eventuality should be formulated if any likelihood of its occurrence appears.

No employee should be sent overseas for more than brief temporary duty without an employment contract. The agreement should spell out the length of the assignment, base salary and overseas premium pay, income tax equalization payments, housing and living allowances, children's education allowances, hours of work, home leave and rest and recreation provisions, transportation of household goods, and termination provisions. A well-drawn contract tells employer and employee where each stands and avoids future problems.

International Federation of Consulting Engineers (FIDIC)

FIDIC is the international federation of national associations of consulting engineers representing the profession in their respective countries. The U.S. member is American Consulting Engineers Council, represented to FIDIC by its FIDIC Liaison Committee.

FIDIC encourages its member associations to adopt and enforce rules of professional conduct in keeping with the responsibility and integrity of the consulting profession and is an effective voice in the international consulting engineering market. It represents its member associations collectively at the international level, cooperates with other international organizations on matters of concern to consulting engineers, and endeavors to enhance the services offered by them. In this connection, it acts as a central source of information on matters of mutual interest to its member associations and publishes a variety of useful material for engineers practicing in the international field.

One of these publications, the *Consulting Engineers Guide to International Agencies,* already has been mentioned. Other publications include model forms of agreement between consulting engineer and client for preinvestment studies and for design and provision of services during construction. FIDIC also publishes *Standard Conditions of Contract for Works of Civil Engineering Construction,* and for electrical and mechanical work, as well as committee reports on such subjects as professional liability and the role of governments in the export of consulting services. A complete list of FIDIC publications, with prices, may be obtained from:

> **FIDIC Secretariat**
> P. O. Box 17334
> 2505 CH
> The Hague
> The Netherlands

Chapter

AMERICAN CONSULTING ENGINEERS COUNCIL

Samuel Adams Bogen
President, Bogen Jenal Engineers, P.C.

The members of most professions in the United States and in other free societies have formed voluntary organizations to protect and advance their interests. Although some may think that such organizations are self-serving, the members of the professions generally see their activities as advancing the public interest as well as their own. Two business problems that have plagued consulting engineers for 10 years or more, and their ultimate resolution, demonstrate how concerted efforts by the professions can benefit both themselves and the public.

The Problem of Professional Competition

How consulting engineers are chosen for work contracted out by public agencies is an example of one problem solved by the organized activity of the consulting engineering profession. In the past, it was not unusual for the head of an agency to contact a local politician for a recommendation. But there were risks involved; the recommended firm might be qualified or it might not. If not, it would be the agency head who was fired, not the politician. If the project, a bridge, for example, failed, the loss of his job was only the beginning of the agency head's problems.

Another method was to select the firm that had previously designed bridges for the agency. That was not too bad a solution, but it did exclude other qualified firms from consideration, perhaps younger ones with fresh ideas.

Another approach was to take bids and give the job to the lowest bidder. But suppose that the lowest bidder had never designed a bridge before, or that the bridges it had designed were so costly to build and maintain that total life-cycle costs, including the low cost of engineering, were higher than for bridges designed by more expensive firms. Perhaps the bridges were unsuited to the site or not up to the current state of the art.

Faced with these selection problems, American Consulting Engineers Council (ACEC), with the help of Congressman Jack Brooks of Texas, developed the concept of competitive negotiation. This was embodied in Public Law 92-582, known as the Brooks Law, which was passed by Congress in 1972. Since then 20 states have enacted similar laws governing selection of engineers and architects for work financed by the state.

How are selections made under the rules of competitive negotiation? First, each major federal project to be designed is advertised in *Commerce Business Daily (CBD)*, published five times a week by the U.S. Department of Commerce. Anyone may subscribe for a small fee. Many engineering firms assign an employee or principal to scan *CBD* every day and respond to projects in the firm's field of competence. Often, if the project is large and complex, teams of firms will group together to solicit an assignment.

The first step is to submit to the agency that advertised the job a record of the firm's previous projects of the same type and a general listing of the firm's recent work. The agency may receive hundreds of such qualification statements. These are reviewed by a selection committee that chooses a small number of firms, generally three to six, considered best qualified for the specific project. Qualifications may include geographical location of the firm relative to the project, particular people available for the project, workload of the firm, its performance on other projects, and other relevant criteria.

The three to six "short-listed" firms are invited to an interview by the selection committee. They are given a short time, usually an hour, to present evidence of their qualifications, to ask questions of the selection committee, and to answer questions. When all short-listed firms have been interviewed, they are ranked by the selection committee in order of qualification, and the most qualified firm is asked to submit a price for the work and an analysis of how the price was arrived at. This submission is then reviewed by the agency to determine if the price is reasonable, based on their prior experience, and if the price breakdown shows a true understanding of what the agency wants. Generally, the agency and the consulting firm will sit down together and carefully negotiate a price somewhat different from that submitted, based on a clear, mutual understanding of the requirements of the project. The negotiation process eliminates whatever guesswork there may have been in the original proposal.

If the negotiations end successfully, a contract results. If no agreement can be reached, the first firm chosen is dismissed, and the second choice is asked to submit a proposal. It is not in competition with the first firm; that firm has been eliminated. Negotiations continue in this way until a mutually agreeable fee is reached.

Thus, organized consulting engineers have worked with the federal government, and with many state and local governments, to develop a selection procedure that is fair to both sides and to the taxpayers, that gives new firms a chance to compete, that reduces the value of political influence, and that displays the steps in the selection process for all to see.

The Professional Liability Problem

A second problem solved by group action concerns the consulting engineer's liability for injury or financial loss that he may cause to others by professional negligence, or by the negligence of employees for whom the engineer is responsible. The same kind of problem afflicts architects and land surveyors, doctors, dentists, lawyers, and accountants. Two cases of alleged professional negligence that have reached the courts show that consulting engineers, like doctors, can be subjected to improbable lawsuits.

In the first half of the twentieth century, David B. Steinman, a notable bridge engineer, designed the Henry Hudson Bridge over the Harlem River in New York, the Straits of Mackinac Bridge connecting upper and lower Michigan, and many other great bridges all over the world. Ten years after Dr. Steinman died, his estate was sued for a very large sum. What had he done wrong? On a bridge designed 20 years earlier, a handrail that should have been painted annually, but was not, rusted out and gave way, injuring a pedestrian crossing the bridge. The injured person sued the owner, the builder, and the designer. Death did not end Dr. Steinman's liability.

Another example of a negligence claim related to a free-standing sign in front of a supermarket. The structure supporting the sign was designed to withstand the wind load at that location. However, the supermarket chain management used the same structure at another location with different wind conditions without having the original structural engineer, or anyone else, check the design for the new site. The second structure failed, and the engineer was sued for negligent design, although he had not designed it for that location.

Beginning in the 1940s, engineers attempted to solve this problem by interesting general insurance companies in writing policies that paid claims in cases where the engineers were held professionally negligent. This was a reasonable way to solve the problem, but it had a major defect. The insurance companies based their premiums on the total claims volume, expected or actual, plus their own overhead and profit. Premiums therefore rose continually and sharply, with little distinction between firms that were careful and those that were sloppy in their work, or between those designing structures where people often were hurt, such as skilifts, and those where people rarely were hurt, such as libraries.

In 1969, ACEC decided to encourage the formation of an insurance company that would seek ways to reduce the financial hazards of professional practice. A corporation was formed in California, and the members of ACEC voluntarily bought $1 million of stock to start the company, known as Design Professionals Insurance Company (DPIC).

DPIC investigated the causes of professional claims and educated its policyholders, and consulting engineers generally, in techniques for doing more precise work, writing more precise contracts, taking care not to promise the impossible, and conducting themselves in a way that would not escalate every difference of judgment into a lawsuit.

Some precautions that DPIC urges its policyholders to take are:

- Use a written agreement rather than a handshake to define your services and the payments you are to receive.
- Do not guarantee to produce a perfect result; in the real world there are many obstacles to perfection, and some will not be within your control.
- Make certain your estimates are understood by your client to be just that: estimates, not guaranteed costs.

• When you visit a construction project to check that the work conforms to your plans and specifications, make sure your contract does not make you responsible for the safety of all the workers on the site. They are not your employees, and you are not responsible for their methods.

The organization most responsible for the solution of these two problems, and many others of comparable public importance, is ACEC.

However, one area in which the concerted efforts of the professions have been unsuccessful is the protection of their codes of ethics and professional conduct guidelines. As the professions organized formal associations, each association began to evolve a set of standards that members were expected to adhere to. In the engineering profession, these codes and guidelines revolved around the premise that engineers should "hold paramount the safety, health, and welfare of the public in the performance of their professional duties." Prohibitions against competitive bidding for a job, self-laudatory advertising, "free" engineering to get a contract, and supplanting another engineering firm or engineer who already has a contract were some of the provisions in the codes and guidelines, all based on the protection of the public.

In the late 1970s, the U.S. Department of Justice's Antitrust Division judged these and other provisions to be in restraint of trade under the Sherman Act, contending that many genuinely ethical prohibitions were intended to protect the professions rather than the public. The U.S. Supreme Court, although noting that a learned profession cannot be judged on the same basis as a commercial enterprise, ruled nonetheless that such ethical prohibitions, regardless of their merits, constituted unlawful restraint of trade. Other professions similarly found themselves in litigation with the Department of Justice, and they, and the engineering organizations, have removed the contested provisions from their codes and guidelines.

Nonetheless, ACEC continues to play a prominent role, within legal constraints, in establishing and maintaining canons of professional conduct.

Origins of ACEC

Originally named Consulting Engineers Council (CEC), the organization was formed in 1956 by 10 state and municipal groups of independent consulting engineering firms. "Independent" is defined as free of conflicting interests; i.e., the member firms do not manufacture, assemble, or install equipment and they are not construction contractors, developers, or vendors. In addition to engineering, some offer architectural, land surveying, and soil analysis services.

In the 25 years since its formation, the 10 member organizations have become 51, covering every state in the nation and including independent organizations in New York City, Pittsburgh, and Washington, D.C. Each city, state, and regional group has its own requirements for membership, dues, meetings, and officers. Each looks to the interests of the profession and of the public in its state capital and its city halls.

The national organization is a federation of its member societies. Its sole purpose is to attend the profession's national and international interests. Through membership in the *International Federation of Consulting Engineers* (FIDIC), ACEC cooperates with the consulting engineers of other countries in an effort to maintain suitable standards of performance in developing countries around the world.

Services to Members

Services offered by ACEC to its members include publications on every aspect of consulting practice, liaison with other professional engineering societies and construction groups, meetings at which lectures and seminars are offered on subjects generally related to the operation of a consulting firm, a scholarship program for engineering students, and contract documents defining the mutual responsibilities of consulting engineers and their clients.

A major ACEC effort is in the field of government affairs. A political action committee called American Consulting Engineers Political Action Committee (ACEPAC) raises funds from voluntary contributions and distributes them to candidates for federal office who best represent the views and interests of independent professional people. In the 1980 congressional elections, ACEPAC contributed $63,000 to 217 candidates; 183 of these were elected.

Skilled and experienced full-time members of the ACEC staff keep in close touch with members of Congress and their staffs, and with the heads of many federal agencies, to acquaint them with the views and the interests of ACEC's members. This, of course, is lobbying, which is a legitimate and legal part of the American system of government. Skilled lobbyists offer information on the probable effect of a piece of legislation or an agency regulation on people in general and on the organizations they represent in particular. Much legislation today is highly technical, and members of Congress, most of whom are lawyers, cannot be expected to be fully aware of its impact. ACEC's committees and staff help to fill in the gaps in these technical areas. Here, for example, are some ACEC committee assignments at the interface of government and engineers:

- Environment—covering legislation and regulations related to water supply, waste water disposal, solid wastes, and water quality
- Energy—concerned with production and conservation
- Transportation—including air transport, highways, bridges, railroads, subways, buses, and truck transport
- Surface mining—recommends regulations to permit the optimum use of our natural resources, with minimum harm to the environment

Another ACEC division deals with public relations and offers advice on how to inform the public about current engineering projects that solve problems applicable to the general welfare. Since almost everything engineers design—whether it be an airport, bridge, hospital, school, subway, barge canal, sewage treatment plant, power plant, or skyscraper—is useful to the public, this should be a routine task. However, most engineers are reluctant to proclaim their accomplishments publicly, and the public relations department does it for them in a tasteful, professional manner.

ACEC also provides its member firms with services that can be bought more advantageously in large volume. For example, major medical, dental, hospital, and life insurance, as well as a portable pension plan, are offered to member firms on a voluntary basis. About one-half of the firms are enrolled. Other firms, particularly the very large ones, are able to negotiate favorable terms directly with insurance companies.

Awards Programs

ACEC runs a variety of awards programs, offering recognition to outstanding engineering achievements and to individuals for notable accomplishments or distinguished service. The Fellows of ACEC, a group of approximately 400 members who have made significant contributions to the profession, present the annual Award of Merit to a member of the engineering profession who may or may not be a member of ACEC or even a consulting engineer. The most recent awards have been given to Lt. Gen. John W. Morris, retired chief of engineers of the U.S. Army Corps of Engineers; Jerome B. Weisner, president of Massachusetts Institute of Technology; James A. Van-Allen, head of the department of physics and astronomy at the University of Iowa; David Packard, cofounder and chairman of the board of Hewlett-Packard Company; Arthur J. Fox, Jr., editor of *Engineering News-Record;* and William H. Pickering, professor of electrical engineering at the California Institute of Technology.

A $10,000 honor award is presented biennially to an individual responsible for a notable new process, device, or program in a selected field. The 1979 honor award, for example, was given to Michael Pope, P.E., of Pope, Evans and Robbins, a New York City consulting firm, for development of the atmospheric fluidized bed combustion process, which permits nonpolluting, economical combustion of a wide variety of low-grade fuels.

ACEC also conducts a national engineering excellence awards competition each year, resulting in the selection of a Grand Conceptor Award for the project built in the course of the previous year that best exemplifies the use of trained professional imagination for a constructive public purpose. Some 15 runner-up, or honor awards, also are presented. Selections are made by committees of prominent people in fields related to engineering who are not members of ACEC.

Other Professional Associations

While ACEC is unique in its structure and concept, there are many other associations that serve the engineering profession. The four oldest and largest, the Founder Societies, are American Society of Civil Engineers (ASCE), American Society of Mechanical Engineers (ASME), American Institute of Mining and Metallurgical Engineers (AIMME), and the Institute of Electrical and Electronic Engineers (IEEE). Each of these societies deals with specific technical branches of engineering. They are headquartered in the United Engineering Center in New York City, which has meeting rooms, dining facilities, and a comprehensive engineering library. Membership is by individual rather than by firm, as is the case with ACEC. Grades of membership generally include Student, Associate, Member, Fellow, or Life member, in progressive order.

Other technical societies pursue the specialties indicated by their names, such as the American Society of Heating, Refrigeration and Air-Conditioning Engineers (ASHRAE), and the Illuminating Engineering Society (IES). All of these groups make important contributions to engineering practice. They develop technical standards and guides that are extremely useful to consulting engineers in the performance of their jobs. They publish journals that record new developments in the field and that carry advertising material with information of new products. They conduct technical meetings at which young engineers can add to their knowledge, meet others engaged in comparable work, and learn of new job opportunities.

Another unique organization in the engineering profession is the National Society of Professional Engineers (NSPE), founded in 1932 by the same D. B. Steinman whose professional liability problem was discussed earlier. Membership in NSPE is open exclusively to individuals registered as professional engineers in one of the 50 states, the District of Columbia, or Puerto Rico. Engineers in training, who have passed two parts of the three-part P.E. license examination, may become associate members.

NSPE members engage in a wide variety of work, as is reflected in the society's five divisions: Professional Engineers in Industry (PEI), Professional Engineers in Education (PEE), Professional Engineers in Government (PEG), Professional Engineers in Construction (PEC), and Professional Engineers in Private Practice (PEPP). While each of these divisions is homogeneous in itself, they frequently have different, and sometimes opposing, interests. For example, PEPP members want government work awarded to consulting firms, while PEG members would like more government work done in-house. Such a conflict sometimes thwarts effective action on the part of NSPE, while ACEC members share a single purpose.

ACEC differs from the other societies in that its membership consists of engineering firms rather than individuals, and they all are engaged solely in the practice of consulting engineering. The council is governed by a board of directors, with one director for each member organization. However, voting strength is based upon the number and size of the firms in each organization. The board meets twice a year to determine the policies, programs, and dues of the council. Between board meetings, the business of ACEC is conducted by an executive committee of national officers and by its permanent, full-time staff, which maintains headquarters in Washington, D.C.

Most of the individuals in ACEC firms are members of NSPE and one or more of the technical societies as well. Such multiple membership represents no conflict, since each group serves a different purpose, and all are worthy of support.

Spirit of Cooperation

Close relationships are maintained with NSPE, AIA, and ASCE. While these relationships usually are cooperative and cordial, each of the other societies has members whose interests may be opposed to those of ACEC's members. Even where there are no conflicting interests, there sometimes are differences in approach that limit cooperation. But on the whole, there is a spirit of friendly competition existing among the professional societies. They may duplicate or compete with one another in such matters as provision of health and life insurance and professional liability insurance, provision of information on federal laws, distribution of manuals that are helpful in conducting a professional practice, conduct of useful seminars, and support of committees that help the groups as a whole to keep abreast of national developments, but they also complement one another for the benefit of all.

These professional societies often cooperate when no one group has the strength to do an effective job for the entire profession. An example of such collaboration is the Committee on Federal Procurement of Architect-Engineer Services (COFPAES). This committee was formed in 1967 by ACEC, ASCE, NSPE, AIA, and American Road and Transportation Builders Association (ARTBA) to monitor federal laws, policies, and procedures governing federal and state procurement of architectural and engineering services. The Brooks Act mentioned earlier was a product of the collaboration of the five organizations in COFPAES.

The member organizations of ACEC also serve the function of bringing competitors together in a spirit of friendship, generally at a lunch or dinner meeting, a golf outing, or a technical seminar. The New York (City) Association of Consulting Engineers (NYACE), for example, holds a monthly luncheon for its members. Some member firms with particular skills in marketing their services may be asked to give a series of lectures on how to sell engineering services. It may seem unlikely that they would share their secrets of success with the competition, but they do, motivated by professional pride and goodwill.

The wonder and the glory of the professions in the United States is that competitors do share their knowledge and their facilities with each other, not in collusion, but in collaboration and the spirit of helpfulness. The feeling seems to be that there is enough work to keep us all occupied for the foreseeable future, and the broadening of each one's knowledge can do only good for the profession as a whole.

For a list of prospective employers in a particular location, write or phone the nearest ACEC member organization, or the national headquarters. Some member organizations will be able to sort out the names by discipline, e.g., mechanical, electrical, civil, or structural, or they may be able to send you a roster of firms with a brief description of the specialties of each. The national headquarters is:

American Consulting Engineers Council
1015 15 Street, N. W.
Washington, D. C. 20005
(202) 347-7474

The 49 member association headquarters and their executive directors are:

CEC of Alabama
R. A. Groenendyke
2416 Scepter Lane
Birmingham, AL 35226
205-979-3498

CEC of Alaska
Charles E. Torkko
CH2M. Hill
2550 Denali Street
Anchorage, AK 99503
907-278-2551

CEC of Arizona
William A. Sawyer
3625 North 16th Street
Phoenix AZ 85016
602-266-4926

ACEC of Arkansas
Major LeRoy Nix, Jr.
Medical Arts Building, Suite 618
1124 Marshall
Little Rock, AR 72202

Consulting Engineers Association of California
John E. Beebe
433 Airport Boulevard, Suite 303
Burlingame, CA 94010
415-344-5782

CEC of Colorado
Sandy Smith
1111 South Colorado Boulevard
Suite 305
Denver, CO 80222
303-757-3379

Consulting Engineers in Private Practice, Connecticut
Richard J. Yedziniak
2600 Dixwell Avenue
Hamden, CT 06514
203-281-4322

CEC of Delaware
William E. Carew, Jr.
Carew Associates, Inc.
2005 Concord Pike
Wilmington, DE 19803
302-658-4281

Florida Institute of Consulting Engineers
Dan Simmons
P. O. Box 750
125 South Gadsden Street
Tallahassee, FL 32302
904-224-7121

CEC of Georgia
Harvey R. Brown
2 Northside 75, Suite 214
Beta Building
Altanta, GA 30318
404-351-3930

CEC of Hawaii
Joyce Haupt
345 Queen Street, Suite 402
Honolulu, HI 96813
808-533-2263

Consulting Engineers of Idaho
Jackie Fuller
842 LaCassia Drive
Boise, ID 83705
208-345-1730

CEC of Illinois
Lonnie H. Carter
220 East Cook Street
P. O. Box 1604
Springfield, IL 62705
217-528-7414

Consulting Engineers of Indiana
Thomas V. McComb
222 North New Jersey, Suite 200
Indianapolis, IN 46204
317-637-3563

CEC of Iowa
David G. Scott
2900 Westown Parkway, Suite 2
West Des Moines, IA 50265
515-225-7966

Kansas Consulting Engineers
George Barbee
803 Merchants National Bank
Topeka, KS 66612
913-357-1824

CEC of Kentucky
Walker R. Reynolds, Jr.
P. O. Box 458
Kentucky Engineering Center
Frankfort, KY 40602
502-695-5680

CEC of Louisiana
Warren J. Wilder
P. O. Box 1549
Baton Rouge, LA 70821
504-387-0843

Consulting Engineers of Maine
Judith W. Harvie
One Middle Street
Hallowell, ME 04347
207-623-1218

CEC of Maryland
Jim Otradovec
3 East Franklin Street
Baltimore, MD 21202
301-539-1592

ACEC of New England
Susan Albert
80 Boylston Street, Suite 1110
Boston, MA 02116
617-482-8835

CEC of Metropolitan Washington
John P. Bachner
8811 Colesville Road, Suite 225
Silver Spring, MD 20910
301-588-6616

CEC of Michigan
Stephen M. Wagner
1407 South Harrison Road, Suite 305
East Lansing, MI 48823
517-332-2066

CEC of Minnesota
Earl G. Oxley
5009 Excelsior Boulevard, Suite 126
Minneapolis, MN 55416
612-922-9696 and 612-927-8705

CEC of Mississippi
Shirley Smith
c/o Cooke-Douglass-Farr
836 Medical Plaza
Jackson, MS 39206
601-373-3428

CEC of Missouri
Wendell E. Locke
P. O. Box 401
Jefferson City, Missouri 65102
314-635-4526

CEC of Montana
Stan Meyer
Wendt Advertising Agency
P. O. Box 2128
Great Falls, MT 59403
406-452-8581

ACEC of Nebraska
Fred E. Anderson, Jr.
7701 Pacific Street, Room 311
Omaha, NE 68114
402-397-1773

CEC of Nevada
Karsten T. Bronken
Karsten T. Bronken Consulting
Engineers
1818 Industrial Road
Las Vegas, NV 89102
702-382-6660

CEC of New Jersey
Peter Allen
66 Morris Avenue
Springfield, NJ 07081
201-379-1100

CEC of New Mexico
Carl Albach
P. O. Box 4235
Santa Fe, NM 87501
505-471-3281

New York Association of Consulting Engineers
R. Joan Faherty
60 East 42nd Street
New York, NY 10017
212-682-6336

CEC of New York State
Richard C. Fritz
3010 Troy Road
Schenectady, NY 12309
518-795-6833

CEC of North Carolina
John L. Moorhead
P. O. Box 447
Durham, NC 27702
919-688-6137 and 688-6904

North Dakota CEC
Bill Moher
Box 2985
Fargo, ND 58108
701-293-7300

Ohio Association of Consulting Engineers
Paul K. Furney
445 King Avenue
Columbus, OH 43201
614-424-6643

CEC of Oklahoma
Mabel Krank
405 N.W. 15th Street
Oklahoma City OK 73103
405-525-7696

CEC of Oregon
Herb Fischborn
P. O. Box 25082
Portland, OR 97225
503-292-6808

CEC of Pennsylvania
John G. Van Natta, II
22 S. 3rd Street, Suite 408
Harrisburg, PA 17105
717-232-3589

CEC of Greater Pittsburgh
Edward T. Wiesmann
Edward T. Wiesmann, Consulting Engineer
1616 Clark Building, 717 Liberty Avenue
Pittsburgh, PA 15222
412-391-0141

CEC of South Carolina
James McAden
Suite 202, First Citizens Building
P. O. Box 11937

Columbia, SC 29211
802-771-4271

CEC of South Dakota
Ronald G. Schmidt
Schmidt, Schroyer & Colwill, P.C.
Pierre Professional Plaza, Suite 201
P. O. Box 8
Pierre, SD 57501
605-224-0461

CEC of Tennessee
Mary D. Shahan
230 Fourth Avenue North
Nashville, TN 37219
615-254-5759

CEC of Texas
David G. Ford
402 San Jacinto Building
Austin, TX 78701
512-474-1474

CEC of Utah
D. J. Cannon
P. O. Box 11777
Salt Lake City, UT 84147
801-531-8743

ACEC of Vermont
Richard P. Trudell
Trudell Consulting Engineers, Inc.
Route 2A, Box 308

Williston, VT 05495
802-879-6331

CEC of Virginia
Harry W. Kincaid
6924 Lakeside Avenue
Richmond, VA 23228
804-264-0051

CEC of Washington
Jack Morell
909 Tower Building
Seattle, WA 98101
206-623-5936

West Virginia CEC
H. Ben Faulkner
Pentree, Inc.
1120 Kanawha Boulevard
Charleston, WV 25301
304-425-9581

CEC of Wisconsin
Larry Jorgensen
2801 West Beltline Highway, #240
Madison, WI 53713
608-271-4654

Wyoming Association of Consulting Engineers and Surveyors
Jerald B. Crews
2334 Rose Lane
Riverton, WY 82501
307-856-1928

INDEX

ABOUT THE CONTRIBUTORS

About the Editor

Stanley Cohen is editor of *Consulting Engineer* magazine. He has won two Jesse H. Neal Awards for editorial achievement and two Jesse H. Neal Certificates of Merit, as well as awards from the American Society of Business Press Editors and the Society for Technical Communication. Mr. Cohen is the author of two books, *The Game They Played* and *The Man in the Crowd*. He has more than 25 years' experience as an editor, writer, and teacher.

Samuel Adams Bogen

Mr. Bogen was president of American Consulting Engineers Council during the 1968–1969 term. He was chairman of the board of directors of Design Professionals Insurance Company from 1970 to 1972 and president from 1972 to 1975. He is a member of the Institute of Electrical and Electronics Engineers, the Illuminating Engineering Society, and the National Society of Professional Engineers. He is president of Bogen Jenal Engineers, P.C., and vice president of Bogen Johnston Lau & Jenal, P.C., in Albertson, New York. Mr. Bogen is a registered professional engineer in 18 states.

Edward K. Bryant

Mr. Bryant is a former partner of Tippetts-Abbett-McCarthy-Stratton, consulting engineers of New York City. He is a Fellow of American Consulting Engineers Council and a former chairman of its International Engineering Committee; a Life Member of the American Society of Civil Engineers, and a member of the American Arbitration Association, the American Society of International Development, and the Society of Military Engineers. He is former chairman of the United Nations Development Programme Committee of the International Federation of Consulting Engineers and is still active on that committee. In 1980, he received the ACEC Past Presidents' Award "in recognition of significant contributions to the international consulting engineering profession."

Leonard K. Crawford

Mr. Crawford, chairman of the board of Crawford, Murphy & Tilly, Inc., Springfield, Illinois, was president of Consulting Engineers Council in 1965–1966 and is a past president of the Illinois Association of Consulting Engineers. He is a Diplomate of the American Academy of Environmental Engineers; a Life Member of the American Society of Civil Engineers; and a member of the National Society of Professional Engineers, the American Water Works Association, the American Public Works Association, the Water Pollution Control Federation, and the Inter-American Association of Sanitary Engineering. Mr. Crawford is a recipient of the Illinois Award from the Illinois Society of Professional Engineers. He is listed in *Who's Who in America*.

Joseph C. Lawler

Mr. Lawler is chairman of the board and chief executive officer of Camp Dresser & McKee, Inc., in Boston. He is a Fellow of American Consulting Engineers Council and chairman of ACEC's Governmental Affairs Committee. In 1977 he received the NSPE Professional Engineers in Private Practice Award. The American Academy of Environmental Engineers honored him with the Gordon Maskew Fair Award in 1979. Mr. Lawler is a member of the National Academy of Engineering.

William W. Moore

Mr. Moore is the founding partner of Dames & Moore, consultants in applied earth sciences, San Francisco. He was president of Consulting Engineers Council in 1964–1965, president of the International Federation of Consulting Engineers in 1970–1972, and vice president of the American Society of Civil Engineers in 1976–1978. He is a Fellow of the Institution of Civil Engineers (England) and a member of the National Academy of Engineering. He received ACEC's Special American Bicentennial Amicus Award in 1976.

William R. Ratliff

Mr. Ratliff is president of American Consulting Engineers Council for the 1981–1982 term. He is a past president of Consulting Engineers Council of Texas and a member of the American Society of Civil Engineers and the National Society of Professional Engineers. He is owner of Ratliff Company in Mt. Pleasant, Texas, and from 1973 to 1980 was senior vice president of Turner, Collie & Braden, Inc., of Houston, Texas.

Thomas B. Robinson

Mr. Robinson is managing partner of Black & Veatch, consulting engineers of Kansas City, Missouri. He is a member of the National

Academy of Engineering and in 1970–1971 was president of Consulting Engineers Council. He is a Fellow of ACEC and the American Society of Civil Engineers; a Diplomate of the American Academy of Environmental Engineers; and a member of the American Society of Mechanical Engineers, the National Society of Professional Engineers, the American Water Works Association, and the Water Pollution Control Federation, among others. Mr. Robinson was assisted in the preparation of his chapter by other members of his firm. They are Paul D. Haney, Henry H. Benjes, Virgil H. Snell, Walter D. Trueblood, Joel P. Kesler, Lester C. Webb, and David H. Lillard.

Richard H. Stanley

Mr. Stanley is president and chief executive officer of Stanley Consultants, Inc., international consultants in Muscatine, Iowa. He is past chairman of the Committee on Federal Procurement of Architectural and Engineering Services (COFPAES); past president of American Consulting Engineers Council, 1976–1977; past president of the Iowa Engineering Society; past chairman of the National Construction Industry Council; member and past chairman of the Engineering College Advisory Council of Iowa State University; and a member of NSPE, ASME, ASCE, IEEE, and other societies. Among his many awards are the Diamond Jubilee Award from the American Society of Mechanical Engineers and the John Dunlap-Sherman Woodward Award from the Iowa Engineering Society.

Eugene B. Waggoner

Mr. Waggoner, a consulting engineering geologist, has been in practice as a private consultant for the past seven years. Prior to that, he was a member of the geotechnical firm, Woodward-Clyde Consultants in San Francisco. He is a Fellow of ACEC and was president of the Council in 1961–1962. He also is a Fellow of the American Society of Civil Engineers and the Association of Soil and Foundation Engineers. Among his many affiliations are his memberships in the Consulting Engineers Association of California, the American Institute of Civil Engineers, the Association of Engineering Geologists, and the U.S. Commission on Large Dams.

C. Richard Walter

Mr. Walter is president of the New York City consulting firm of Hazen and Sawyer, P.C. He is a past president of the New York Association of Consulting Engineers and a former national director of ACEC and the Water Pollution Control Federation. He is serving as a trustee of the Consulting Engineers Life/Health Insurance Plan and the Engineering Foundation.